WITH STANLEY ON THE CONGO BY M. DOUGLAS

LONDON, EDINBURGH,
DUBLIN, AND NEW YORK
THOMAS NELSON
AND SONS

CONTENTS.

LIST OF ILLUSTRATIONS.

———◆◆———

WITH
STANLEY ON THE CONGO.

CHAPTER I.

A NEW SCHEME.

ONE day in the month of January 1878 two
gentlemen stood on the platform of the railway
station at Marseilles, awaiting the arrival of the
Italian express. They had been sent by Leopold the
Second, King of the Belgians, to meet a man whose
name at that time was ringing through Europe—Henry
Morton Stanley, who, a few years previously, had
"found" Livingstone in the wilds of Africa. Stanley
was now homeward bound, after having crossed the
African continent from east to west, and traced the
great river Congo from Lake Tanganyika to the spot
where it discharged its waters into the broad Atlantic.
The tidings of the discovery of a great water-way to
the very heart of Africa had already been noised
abroad; and even before the pioneer of the route
had set foot in Europe, busy brains had begun to

plan ways and means to take advantage of the new field of enterprise thus laid open. First and foremost among the planners was Leopold of Belgium, who, determined to take time by the forelock, had dispatched his commissioners to meet Stanley, and bespeak his co-operation and help in the great scheme.

Travel-worn, weary, and broken in health as Stanley was, he could not brook the idea of returning to Africa. Advice he was willing to give, but to lead another expedition!—no, that was out of the question, at any rate for the time being. But a few months' rest so entirely changed his views of life that November of the same year found him at Brussels in conference with King Leopold and several influential gentlemen, who had come from various parts of Europe to consider the best means of opening up the Congo region. Questions fairly showered on Stanley, the only man in Europe who could answer them. How much of the Congo was navigable? What view of commercial enterprise might the chiefs on its banks be expected to take? What tribute would they be likely to demand from traders? What were the productions of the region? These and other queries were propounded in rapid succession, and though some were unanswerable offhand, the result of the conference was so far satisfactory that £20,000 towards the proposed enterprise was subscribed in the room. A " Committee of Study of the Upper Congo " was also formed; and Stanley, whose vigour and activity were completely re-established, was appointed leader and commander of the expedition which was to carry out the objects of the Committee. His duties were to include the establishment of trading-stations at various convenient points, and to lease or purchase a suitable tract of ground around each station, and also, if desirable, along the connecting trade routes.

The preliminary arrangements were rapidly concluded, and by the beginning of February 1879 Stanley was making his way to Zanzibar on board the steamer *Albion*, which had been chartered by the Committee for the purposes of the expedition. At Zanzibar he enlisted *pagazis*, or porters, and performed various duties whilst awaiting the arrival of another steamer, the *Barza*, with other members of the expedition, and a cargo of stores for their use. These miscellaneous occupations included sending letters of advice and instruction to sundry officers who, during the time that Stanley had spent in Equatorial Africa, had been sent to Unyanyembe and elsewhere to establish trading-stations, make scientific observations, study native languages and customs, as far as possible suppress the slave trade, and otherwise endeavour to open up the country and form friendly relations with the natives.

All this work occupied some time, but towards the end of May the *Albion*, with Stanley, his secretary Mr. Swinburne, his black companions—many of whom had been with him on his recent journey down the Congo—and an assortment of stores, sailed for the Congo, *viâ* the Red Sea and Mediterranean route. Some slight delay was occasioned on the way by an accident to part of the machinery, which compelled the *Albion* to call at Sierra Leone ; but the interruption was pleasant rather than otherwise, and on August 14th Stanley arrived at Banana Point, the Dutch trading-station at the mouth of the Congo.

The view from the sea as the steamer approached was not very inspiring. A long line of low, red cliffs rose from the shore to an expanse of sloping land thinly clothed with parched-up grass, varied here and there by clumps of trees. Farther to the south lay a forest area, bounded on the north and south by hill ridges ; and through the centre of this flowed the mighty Congo to its resting-place in the blue Atlantic. By degrees, as the *Albion* approached, the great river disclosed itself, dividing the forest into two sections, and stretching away for miles like a broad silver streak under the blaze of sunshine.

Then out came the pilot—a fine big fellow, who for years had lived on the low sand-spit known as Banana Point—and in another hour the *Albion*, her voyage at an end, lay snugly at anchor near the Dutch factory. Here she was speedily boarded by the officers of the expedition—five Belgians, two Englishmen, two Danes, an American, and a Frenchman —who had arrived some time before in the *Barza*.

For a time Stanley was fully occupied in greeting and comparing notes with his future companions; but his attention had soon to be turned to other matters, for the *Barza* had brought a full cargo of stores, and these, as well as a small fleet of river steamers moored near the Dutch factory, awaited his inspection.

For seven days the expedition remained at Banana Point, enjoying the hospitality of the Dutch employés, who doubtless welcomed a little variety in their somewhat monotonous lives. They lived well, it is true; but to young fellows, as almost without exception they were, neither the daily round at the factory nor the natural features of Banana Point can have been very exciting. The point itself—a low, sandy promontory, protected against the inroads of sea and river by stakes, piles, and imported rocks—nowhere rose more than twelve feet above high water-mark, and apparently had been named in accordance with the rule of contrary, for not a single banana plant was visible. On the seaward side the Atlantic waves dashed restlessly against the firm white sand. Landward the view was bounded by the mudbanks and mangrove swamps of Banana Creek.

The factory itself, with its storehouses and numerous employés, white and black, was busy enough. There men-of-war and mail steamers called to coal; natives from all the country round came to barter their palm oil and other produce for gunpowder, cutlery, firearms, cast-off military coats, or the hundred and one other articles with which the traders sought to attract them; while Kruboys and other labourers noisily performed the multitude of miscellaneous duties incidental to the station.

Amid this scene of activity Stanley and his companions were not idle. First, there were a few minor difficulties to be adjusted among the officers, several of whom found ground of complaint: one demanding higher pay, a second higher rank, a third objecting to his messmates, a fourth aspiring to fame, honour, and the post of second in command; while almost everybody pressed claims for wine, board and lodging, tobacco, and clothing, free, gratis, and all for nothing. To all these complaints Stanley had to attend; and when they were satisfactorily settled, a new difficulty arose in the discovery of a number of imperfections among the steamers. Some merely required a few minor alterations; but one, the *En Avant*, a paddle-boat of six horse-power, performed extraordinary freaks, and drove her engineers to the verge of despair before one of them, an Italian named Flamini, discovered that her vagaries were due to slight defects in her machinery.

By August 27th the last preparations were completed, and on the morning of that day the fleet began the voyage up the tawny waters of the Congo. On either shore nature seemed to be asleep; the mudbanks, the mangrove swamps, the wooded shores, were alike silent. On the broad expanse of the great river the only sound that broke the stillness was the throbbing of the engines of the boats.

Four hours' steaming brought the expedition to Ponta da Lenha, or Wood Point—not a very distinctive title, seeing that almost every foot, both of banks and islands, was densely forested. Here there was another Dutch settlement; and as the vagaries of the *En Avant* had left her far behind the rest of the flotilla, Stanley decided to halt. In the morning the missing boat was still conspicuous by her absence; so, leaving her to follow at her leisure, the expedition pushed forward to Boma, the principal European trading-station on the Congo.

From Boma, where Stanley engaged the services of De-de-de, a chief who had befriended him on his last expedition, the *Albion* steamed on to Mussako, four hours farther up-stream. Here the landing-place proved so convenient that Stanley promptly decided to bring up all his stores, and form a temporary base. Orders were given to discharge the cargo; and while the work was in progress, Stanley, with Captain Thompson of the *Albion*, took the steam lifeboat *Royal*, and reconnoitred the river above Mussako. But, ignorant as they were of the proper course to steer, the current simply played with the boat, tossed her about like a cork, and finally drove her back ignominiously towards the camp. The disappointed navigators then decided to look for hippopotami, and Stanley showed Thompson one of the huge creatures calmly reposing in the water, with his head resting on the bank. Thompson, however, flatly refused to believe that the object pointed out to him had any connection with a hippo, and when no movement followed the discharge of an Express rifle, aimed point-blank at the ungainly object, he laughed Stanley to scorn for having, as he declared, "fired at a rock." But when he had landed and made personal inspection of the slaughtered hippo, he was forced to admit his error, and atone for various gibes by many compliments addressed to the amused and triumphant sportsman.

For about a fortnight all hands were kept busy in fetching, unloading, and safely bestowing the stores; but at length the not over-agreeable task was completed, and the *Albion* started on her homeward voyage. So far not an hour's pioneering work had been done; but only one factory—at Nokki—lay above Mussako, and beyond that point it was doubtful whether a steamer could ascend, as the rocky banks closed in upon the river, forming a comparatively narrow cañon, through which the stream rushed like a mill race. One navigator indeed—Captain Tuckey, who in 1816 was detailed by the Admiralty to explore the Congo—safely negotiated the cañon; but near Vivi, a little farther up-stream, he lost his life in a whirlpool. Thenceforward the Congo above Nokki had been left

severely alone, and to Stanley, therefore, remained
the honour of opening up the navigation. By dint
of hugging the southern bank, and watching every
curve of the shore and swirl of the current, the
steamers passed safely through the cañon, and
anchored at the mouth of the river Lufu, which
bounded the rocky district of Vivi. Farther than
this Stanley did not consider it prudent to ascend;
and, moreover, his friend De-de-de assured him that
there was an excellent site for a station in the immediate neighbourhood.

It was too late to make a detailed investigation
that day, and notwithstanding De-de-de's assurances, Stanley felt considerable doubts as to the
suitability of the spot for his purpose. Still, as
there was certainly the possibility that what the
chief said was correct, Stanley decided to make an
inspection. Early on the following morning he accompanied De-de-de to a hill above the camp, whence
the chief pointed out a safe channel up the rushing, tumultuous stream. As he further professed an
entire acquaintance with the navigation, Stanley
consented to let him pilot the steamer *Esperance*
up the channel, and within a few minutes the little
boat was working her way up the Congo with dangers
on either hand. To the right the water boiled,
heaved, and raged in a series of whirlpools and
rapids; while on the left a line of rocky islets threatened destruction to any unfortunate craft that the

furious stream might hurl upon them. But perilous
as it looked, the passage was safely accomplished,
and the *Esperance*, leaving the rapids astern, reached
a safe anchorage near a sandy beach, from which
a precipitous cliff reared its rocky face to a level
plateau three hundred feet above.

To the eastward the cliff was inaccessible, and on
the landward side of the spur, which formed the
plateau, the ground rose abruptly to a rocky emi-
nence, whose castle-like summit promptly gained for
it the title of Castle Hill. But on the westward the
spur, though steep, was climbable, and it was on
the natural fortress thus formed that De-de-de proposed to found the first station. To Stanley, however, the idea seemed almost absurd, for to his
unaccustomed eyes the place looked like a wilderness
of hills and rocks, fronted by a turbulent river, and
backed by forests of unknown extent. Still he was
willing to be taught, and having, at De-de-de's
suggestion, fired the high grass, so as to clear the
way to the plateau, he sat down to breakfast.

By the time the meal was finished the flames had
done their work, and, guided by the chief, he climbed
the toilsome ascent to the plateau. To the eastward lay another and larger plateau, while inland
the Castle Hill towered at least six hundred feet
above him. Altogether the spot was not by any
means all that Stanley's fancy had painted for the
site of his first and main station.

"To be, or not to be?" And while he was turning over the pros and cons a party of natives from the village called Chinsalla, which occupied a fertile hollow on the larger plateau, came to see the white man who had suddenly appeared in their district. They were manifestly friendly, and their amiability, combined with the obvious healthiness and defensibility of the plateau, turned Stanley's decision in its favour—provided, of course, that easy access both from the sea and the interior could be assured. As these points could only be ascertained by careful investigation, after visiting Chinsalla and sending messengers to summon the five chiefs of Vivi district to a palaver that evening, Stanley proceeded to survey the plateau, and take careful soundings in the river. These investigations kept him fully occupied for several hours; but the results were satisfactory, and about four o'clock in the afternoon he returned to his camp to meet the chiefs and open negotiations with them.

At the appointed hour they made their appearance, attired in a curious mixture of native and European clothing. Two wore cast-off military tunics, a third was gorgeous in a discarded livery coat, while the others were more soberly clad—one in a brown and one in a black coat. All wore native loin-cloths instead of trousers, and the majority were decorated with anklets and bracelets of brass wire. Their followers, who were armed with " Tower "

flint-lock muskets, were dressed in native style, with
striped cotton caps or felt or straw hats, according
as their fancy dictated.

When all were seated the palaver was opened by
Massala, the linguist or spokesman of Chinsalla, who,
in the name of all the chiefs, formally welcomed
the *mundele*, or trader—a term applied in that
locality to all whites—to Vivi. Stanley returned
thanks, and then proceeded to explain his wants—
namely, land on which to build a station, and the
right to make roads on which all men, white and
black, might go to and fro unmolested. He further
suggested that the chiefs should retire to talk over
his proposition, and return on the following day
with their answer. To this they agreed, and having
begged a bottle of gin apiece, retired with De-de-de
to consider the matter.

On the following day, when the palaver was resumed, Massala informed Stanley that they were
willing to grant any unoccupied land that the *mundele* might select for his station ; he might build as
many houses and make as many roads as he pleased ;
he should be the sole *mundele* of Vivi, and without
his permission no other white man should be permitted to set foot in the district. The people of
Vivi should have full permission to work for him
in any capacity. Immunity from molestation was
guaranteed to all and sundry of his employés ; and
in the event of any disagreement between the strangers

and the people of Vivi, the chiefs promised that the complaint should be laid before the *mundele*. For all these concessions some equivalent was, of course, expected, and after a considerable time spent in bargaining, Stanley agreed to pay a monthly rent of £2—or, rather, of cloth to that value—and also a cash-down sum of £32 worth of cloth. The price was rather high as values went, but as no better terms could be obtained an agreement was forthwith drawn up and signed by all the parties concerned.

CHAPTER II.

THE FIRST STATION.

TO obtain the concession was one thing, to found the station was another; and when Stanley inspected his chosen site, he was forced to confess to himself that the difficulties in his way were legion. The first thing necessary was to construct a road from the landing-place to the plateau, and as this could not be done without men, tools, provisions, and materials, the steamer *Esperance* was kept busy for some days in bringing men and stores from Mussako.

Early on October 1st the road was begun, and the chiefs of Vivi, with their people, turned out in force to watch the operations. As they stood gazing in open-eyed wonder an idea occurred to Stanley: there was much to be done, and he had but a hundred men—why should not the people of Vivi lend a hand, instead of standing idly watching?

Approaching the chiefs he introduced the subject, making judicious reference to the bales of cloth, bright-coloured handkerchiefs, beads, and ornaments in his stores at the landing-place. Would they not like to possess them ? If so, let them set to work to clear the plateau; and then at night, when the wages earned during the day were paid, a jar of good rum—a luxury much appreciated on the Congo —should be thrown into the bargain.

To work for wages ! The idea was a new and delightful one, at first hardly credible to men who among their own people had never been paid for their labour. It seemed too good to be true ; but when, after much consideration and discussion, they ventured to believe it, they wasted less time than usual in bargaining, and soon sixty - five men, women, and children were busily at work clearing the plateau of stones and scrub. So far Stanley was the only European at Vivi, for the others were all engaged elsewhere with the stores and boats ; he had therefore to supervise everything himself. But work went on merrily, and such good progress was made that by October 13th, though the road was not yet fit for wheeled traffic, goods could be carried up to the plateau. About this time, too, the European staff began to arrive, and the work of bringing up the stores and materials was pushed forward with renewed energy. No sooner was a cargo unloaded at the landing-place than gangs of men shouldered the goods, and thus, section by section, frame-houses, iron-work, and other necessaries were laboriously transported to the plateau, where the industrious

natives had made a clean sweep of rocks, scrub, and
rubbish. A few boulders too large to be handled
still remained, and Stanley disposed of these by
setting a gang to work with crowbars and hammers,
to smash the rocks and hurl the fragments down
the hill. His own prowess with the sledge-hammer,
as he instructed the men in the use of that somewhat unwieldy implement, so greatly impressed the
natives that, with the African love of bestowing
nicknames, they forthwith dubbed him Bula Matari
—that is, Breaker of Rocks.

A plan for the new settlement had been drawn
out, and in accordance with this the carpenter and
his crew proceeded to erect a series of wooden huts,
while one of the engineers superintended the construction of iron storehouses. Other men were set
to work to excavate a shallow hollow in the centre
of the plateau, the dry, sun-baked earth they removed being used to level up inequalities, especially
at the river end of the plateau, which was so rough
and rocky that the only way of dealing with it was
to build a low wall at the edge of the plateau, and
fill up the space behind it with stones and rubbish.
A force of Vivi natives meanwhile was detailed to
carry up rich black soil from the fertile Nkusu
valley, bounding the eastern side of the plateau.
This soil was dumped in the central excavation, and
thus, after about three weeks' work, a garden plot
was made ready for the reception of sundry fruit

trees and vegetable seeds brought by Stanley for
the purpose. Aided by careful watering, these flour-
ished amazingly, and speedily justified the trouble
expended on them.

A residence for the chief of the station still had
to be provided. As the site for this Stanley selected
the terrace at the river end of the plateau, and here
he built a substantial two-storied house, using for
the purpose some big balks of timber originally des-
tined for the construction of a dry dock.

By the middle of February 1880, matters were so
far advanced that Stanley handed over the care of the
station to its future chief, Mr. Augustus Sparhawk,
associated with whom were Messrs. J. Kirkbright,
assistant-in-chief; A. H. Moore, storekeeper; A.
B. Swinburne, secretary; and F. Mahoney, whose
duties were not at first defined. Three steamers—
the *Belgique*, *Esperance*, and *En Avant*—were also
attached to the station, with about two hundred
African natives to act as porters, labourers, etc.

Above Vivi the course of the Congo was so broken
by rapids and cataracts that for several miles it was
totally unnavigable. To Isangila, a fairly populous
district, fifty-two miles distant up-stream, where
Stanley proposed to found his next station, it was
therefore necessary that a wagon road should be
constructed. But the country between the two
places was only less difficult than the river : the
construction of a road threatened to be a terrible

task; and on February 21st, Stanley, with an escort of natives, set out to search for a route which did not offer insurmountable obstacles.

Go where he would, however, he first must descend the steep slope from the station plateau. The most promising route lay across the larger plateau to the eastward; so, crossing the fertile Nkusu ravine, the party climbed the steep ascent on the farther side, and after passing through the village of Chinsalla, ascended to the summit of Vivi Mountain, a thousand feet above the station. Here was another village, with well-tilled gardens; but beyond this the path—only a foot or so in width—plunged suddenly into a dense thicket of tall grass rising high above the men's heads, and after meandering for some distance along the crest, made a steep descent to another group of villages, or, as the natives called them, *banzas*.

Leaving the villages the explorers passed along the pleasant valley of the Loa River, and then descended five hundred feet to a fertile plateau, which, however, soon terminated abruptly in another ravine, where they camped for the night at a village called Banza Kimpunzu, pleasantly situated in the grass-clad Muzonzila gorge. In the morning, after ascending the farther side of the gorge, they found themselves on a breezy, *banza*-studded plateau, around which it appeared the Muzonzila gorge wound its way, for later in the day they descended to De-de-de's village, nestling deep down in the serpentine ravine. Here it was necessary to halt, for news of Stanley's approach had already been noised abroad, and from all the villages around the chiefs had sent messengers to inform him that they purposed visiting him. This was equal to an announcement that every chief would expect a present, so, before the expected visitors appeared, stores were overhauled and suitable gifts prepared. When road-making was begun in earnest, the co-operation of all these chiefs would be required; it was therefore only politic to gain their good-will beforehand.

Soon they began to arrive with their followers and their gifts—chiefly goats, fowls, bananas, and palm wine; and when these had been presented to the white man, and greetings had been exchanged, the business of the meeting began. Stanley opened the proceedings by explaining the reason of his presence among them, and in a somewhat lengthy speech told them of his desire to carry a wagon road through their territory, and detailed the various concessions he wished to obtain from them. When he had finished his audience retired to consider the matter, and after a long deliberation returned with their answer. They were of opinion that the proposed road would be an advantage to the country, and were perfectly willing to sell land and allow their people to work for fair wages.

On the day after the palaver, Stanley, again advancing, entered the district through which he and his party, half-famished, weary, and almost hopeless, had struggled so painfully three years before on their journey down the Congo. Then all had looked gloomy and forbidding; but now, in happier circumstances, the very face of nature seemed changed. True, the country was wild and rugged—by no means what a prospective road-maker might picture as an ideal route. But stay, was it necessary to follow the native path over mountain ridges, up and down gorges, and across the intervening plateaus? Stanley thought not, and as he advanced farther, and made more and more careful investigation of the lie of the ground, he came to the conclusion that much labour might be saved by ascending the valleys of the Lufu and Loa Rivers to the Muzonz'la gorge, and then following its windings through the plateaus. But in the meantime he confined himself to the up-hill and down-dale native path, which, after leading him over the rugged Inga plateau, in whose forests and gullies all manner of wild animals made their homes, brought him to the valley of the Bundi River. Thence, after crossing the stream—by no means an easy task, as at that point it flowed through a deep rocky gorge—he pushed on through a series of valleys to the Congo bank, where he halted on a plain rising about forty feet above the level of the water.

Having seen his party safely encamped, Stanley,

with a few picked men, set out to explore the
Congo bank down to the mouth of the Bundi River,
some eighteen miles below the plateau. This took
him through a considerable tract of uninhabited
country, where buffaloes, elephants, and other wild
animals browsed undisturbed by man. Another
interesting discovery was that of a valley running
parallel with the Congo, and evidently in former
days the bed of that river, though how or why the
course had changed was not immediately apparent.
In fact, the scene continually varied. Monotonous
the work certainly was not, but it was fatiguing in
the extreme; and towards sunset, after a hard
struggle to force a path through a dense thicket of
cane, the explorers began to look for a pool or
stream where they might camp for the night.

Neither pool nor stream, however, was visible.
The apology for a path which they had been following now utterly disappeared; black darkness set in,
and man after man exhausted himself in vain endeavours to find or make a road through the thicket.
When many had failed, Mabruki, one of the lads who
had accompanied Stanley on his previous journey
down the Congo, tried his luck, declaring that, though
others had failed, he would certainly succeed. The
canes, however, still proved as stubborn as ever:
again and again he assaulted them, only to retire
discomfited among the jeers of his companions; and
his temper was rapidly rising when, after an extra

vigorous onslaught, he burst through the cane barrier
and disappeared from view.

His comrades, instantly sobered, shouted to him;
and then back came his voice from a deep narrow
gully into which he had fallen. There was water,
he said, at the bottom; but his joy at finding it was
considerably dashed by the fact that in falling he
had broken the gourd which served him as water
bottle. The announcement of his woes once more
raised a laugh at his expense; and when he had been
pulled out of the water-course, the explorers, with
restored good temper, pitched their camp and prepared supper.

On the morrow Stanley rejoined his men, and the
expedition continued its toilsome way across the
rugged, mountainous country to Isangila, memorable
to Stanley as the scene of the camp where, in 1877,
he had been compelled to abandon his boats and
his donkey. On that occasion the chiefs of the
district had not been remarkable for amiability;
Stanley consequently did not expect a very friendly
reception. But now all was changed. With a store
of gifts for the white man, who, as rumour had it,
had already worked such wonders at Vivi, they came
thronging in to hold a palaver, which ended as usual
in the concession of land for a " town," and of all
else that Stanley required.

So far he had every reason to be satisfied with his
discoveries. The country, it is true, was very rugged

and broken; but by a judicious selection of valleys and gorges it would, he saw, be quite feasible at some future time to construct a railway from Vivi to Isangila. Numerous tunnels, cuttings, and bridges would, of course, have to be engineered. But a railway was then scarcely more than a vision, and in the meantime he had to think of a wagon road along which the boats and steamers intended to ply on the Upper Congo might be hauled past the rapids and cataracts that barred the stream between Vivi and Isangila. With a hundred and thirty men, the total force at his disposal, the task would be laborious enough; but the difficulties appeared to be only such as patience and perseverance could conquer, and on March 10th the reconnoitring party went back to Vivi to prepare for the heavy work awaiting them.

CHAPTER III.

" 'TIS DOGGED AS DOES IT."

WHEN the necessary staff had been assigned to Vivi, the force available for pioneering work numbered only a hundred and six men—a mere handful in proportion to the magnitude of the proposed work. But inasmuch as no more were forthcoming, Stanley put a brave face on the matter, and on March 18th he turned his back on Vivi, pitched his camp on the bank of the Loa River, and then proceeded to clear a road through the canelike grass, which in many places was over ten feet in height. His own share of the work consisted in marking out the course with a long cord and a series of white flags, a duty that could only be performed with the aid of a pair of steps high enough to enable the pathfinder to obtain a view of his surroundings. This done, the road-makers, each armed with a sharp Dutch hoe, attacked the grass, working so effectively that by sunset nearly half a mile of roadway fifteen feet wide was cleared.

Farther on the roughness of the ground added to

the difficulty of the undertaking. Here a deep gully had to be filled up; there boulders to be removed or levelled, trees and scrub to be cut down. But Bula Matari was at work, and one by one the obstacles were overcome. Still it was a weary, heartbreaking task; for as food, cloth, tools, and requisites of all descriptions had to be carried or hauled by the men, every foot of the way had to be traversed at least three times. Snakes of various species were frequently encountered, but though many of them were poisonous no one was bitten. Game, too, was fairly plentiful; and as fresh meat was a most desirable addition to the otherwise rather monotonous bill of fare, Stanley undertook the duty of hunter to the party, and, when his other labours were finished, went off with his rifle in search of hartebeest, a kind of antelope whose flesh was voted particularly delicious.

Just over a month's hard labour brought the expedition to Makeya Manguba, a convenient landing-place on the banks of the Congo, about five miles from the confluence of the Bundi River, and twenty two miles from Vivi. From this point the river was navigable for some miles, so road-making was suspended, and the pioneers returned to Vivi, whence, after a few days' rest, they again set out, hauling the steamer *Royal* on a wagon, with the view of launching her at Makeya Manguba. Other carts were loaded with a miscellaneous assortment of goods,

ranging from a boiler to a coil of wire, not to mention tents, baggage, and provisions. Five Europeans
—Mr. Swinburne, two Danish sailors, Martin Martinsen and Albert Christopherson, and the engineers
of the *Royal*—with fifty Vivi natives were added to
the party.

This time, notwithstanding the heavy loads to be
hauled, comparatively rapid progress was made, and
on May 11th the *Royal* was triumphantly launched.
This accomplished, Stanley left the engineers to
superintend the cutting of a supply of wood for fuel,
while he returned to Vivi.

It was not to be expected that an expedition such
as that which Stanley had in hand could be carried
through without losses and difficulties, other than
those due directly to the country and the natives.
The undertaking had attracted sundry Europeans
who had no real fitness, either mental or physical,
for the work: as a natural consequence the gloss
quickly disappeared, and while some fell ill or died,
others became unhappy and discontented. Thus
Mr. Pettit, one of the engineers, had already succumbed ; and several others, finding the work harder
or the discomforts greater than their fancy had
pictured, had resigned their posts during Stanley's
absence. His return was the signal for further
changes, and Mr. Moore, the storekeeper at Vivi,
being unable to stand the climate, was compelled
to go home. Two or three others who did not know

(1,153)

Building the Road at Ngoma Point.

their own minds first resigned, and then withdrew
their resignations.

The work of conveying the boats, machinery, furniture, and other heavy goods, from Vivi to Makeya
Manguba, kept the men fully occupied until the end
of July; and meanwhile death was busy among
them. Martin Martinsen and an Englishman named
Deanes both succumbed; one of the blacks was
snapped up by a crocodile; two fell victims to dysen-
tery; and a number of others were on the sick list
for longer or shorter periods.

The first difficulty with the natives occurred about
the time that the last loads reached Makeya Manguba,
where Mr. Swinburne was then in charge. It was
occasioned by an ill-conditioned chief, who, for some
reason unknown, had taken umbrage at the advent
of the white men. During one of Stanley's absences
at Vivi, he had forbidden his people to trade with
the expedition, and after roundly abusing the Europeans of the party, ended by spitting in their faces.
Shortly after Stanley returned he paid a second
visit, and finding some of his people trading in the
camp, began to knock them about. Stanley's indignation was aroused, and seizing the chief by
the arm, he inquired what was meant by such
conduct.

Instead of answering, the chief raised his hand to
strike; but Stanley was quicker, and administered
a hearty slap on the face before the chief could

touch him. The war was thus carried into the
enemy's camp, and the chief, now thoroughly angry,
sprang to snatch his gun from a man who was carrying it. Before he could fire, however, Stanley's
men, at a word from their leader, seized and bound
the aggressor, whose followers were sent off to
inform the paramount chief of the occurrence,
and demand the payment of a fine for the misconduct of the minor chief. Native law fortunately
ordained that the aggressor in any quarrel, if not
the winner, must pay the penalty; and on the following day, when the senior chief arrived, and the
assault was proved by sundry witnesses, the offender
was condemned to pay a fine of four pigs and four
goats, and to convey personally three letters sepa-
rately to Vivi. Stanley reduced the penalty to one
pig and three goats; and later on, when the letters
had been conveyed and the chief brought to order,
he remitted the fine altogether.

The next camp, on the Bundi River, was accessible
by water, and on August 3rd the boats were loaded
up, and the transport of the goods began. In a
week the transfer was completed, and on August 10th
some of the pioneers set to work to chop a road
through a trackless forest of bombax, guaiacum,
mahogany, and teak. Tree after tree fell before the
fierce onslaught of the woodmen; and whilst they
were busy among the timber, another gang cleared
the path of rocks, filled in the chasms, levelled the

inequalities of the ground, and generally prepared the way for the passage of the wagons.

The food supply now became something of an anxiety; for though a few natives with sweet potatoes, bananas, fowls, and other produce, followed in the track of the expedition, the route lay through an uninhabited wilderness. Mr. Swinburne, who acted as caterer, consequently bought up anything and everything eatable that was offered to him; for as the daily consumption equalled four hundred pounds of rice, or its equivalent, it was very desirable that the commissariat should not be wholly dependent on the supplies brought up from Vivi. For the same reason Stanley put in a good deal of his spare time in hunting, and the game—chiefly hartebeest and buffalo—which he brought in made a welcome variation in the otherwise chiefly vegetable diet. Sometimes, when the supply of meat exceeded the requirements of the camp, the surplus was bartered for fresh vegetables, or, with other gifts, was utilized to induce a few of the natives to enlist themselves as labourers.

A month's hard work brought the expedition to the foot of the steep Nyongena Hill, whose precipitous slopes were thickly strewn with huge boulders. The ascent proved quite as troublesome as it looked; but by dint of persevering labour the difficulty was overcome, and the explorers entered a forest reputed to be haunted by evil spirits given to carrying off intruders into their domains. The natives feared to proceed; but when they saw the Zanzibaris and other strangers boldly attack the trees without feeling any evil consequences, they regained confidence, and wielded their hoes and choppers with their accustomed energy.

The next noteworthy difficulty occurred immediately after crossing the Lulu River, beyond which the ground rose in a remarkably steep ascent. To haul up the heavy wagons in the usual way was out of the question; but an ingenious arrangement of blocks and tackles, worked with the aid of the huge trees growing by the wayside, proved most satisfactory, and in a couple of days boats, machinery, and other baggage were all safe at the top of the hill.

Unfortunately, every obstacle overcome seemed but to open the way for others, and now the Ngoma Mountain loomed ominously ahead. Sweeping round its base was the Congo with its impassable rapids, and in closer proximity to the camp was the deep valley of the Bulu River, which must be traversed before the mountain could be tackled. Altogether the prospect was anything but encouraging.

Sunday, November 7th, was a day of rest for all, and after a stroll down to the Congo, a bath, a shave, and a hearty breakfast, Stanley sat down for a comfortable read. Before long, however, Lutete Kuna, one of his young men, came running up to

him with a scrap of paper bearing the words, "Le
Comte Savorgnan de Brazza, Enseigne de Vais-
seau," hastily inscribed in pencil. As counts are
not to be met every day in Central Africa, and
Stanley had only vaguely heard of the gentleman
in question, who, when he left Europe, was supposed
to be somewhere on the Ogowai, he naturally felt
some surprise; but the messenger was unable to
furnish any satisfactory information. He had met a
tall white man, he said, who claimed to be a Frenchman, and amused himself by firing at the trees.
This mysterious person had entered into conversation with Lutete, and finding that he belonged to
Stanley's party, sent him off with an improvised
visiting card to his master.

M. de Brazza in due time followed his card, and
received a hearty welcome, though, as neither he nor
Stanley could speak much of the other's language,
conversation was carried on under difficulties. It
appeared, however, that he had succeeded in exploring the Ogowai, and had afterwards made his
way from that river to Stanley Pool, whence, travelling seawards, he heard of Stanley, and struck off
to his camp, where he rested for a couple of days.
After his departure the refreshed and rested explorers pushed forward to a sandy flat, beyond which
the Ngoma Mountain made a sheer descent to the
Congo. The mountain appeared impracticable, the
stream unnavigable; what was to be done?

Fairly at his wits' end, Stanley strolled down to view Ngoma Point, where mountain and torrent met. Yes, here was his chance; for the tracks of various animals were plainly marked between the rocks, going on and on towards a wooded terrace visible beyond the point. Where a beast could go a man could follow: but what about the wagons? They could not scramble between the boulders, where there was barely foothold for a goat. Stay, though: why should not those very rocks, which seemed to bar the way, be turned into the means of passing the barrier? By rolling down some large ones into the stream a foundation might be made to carry a wall, which, in its turn, might support a road. It would be stiff work, of course, but not so stiff as hauling the wagons over the mountain; and then and there Stanley decided on the wall.

Trees were cut to act as levers, hard-wood poles for handspikes, and forty of the best men were told off to act as builders, while the rest brought stones from the mountain side. First one big boulder, then another, was dislodged from its resting-place, and hauled and levered to its new position at the margin of the river. In the course of a week a solid foundation was laid; stones were piled one upon another, until at last such a height was reached that, as the mountain sloped away from the stream, sufficient width had been gained to allow of the passage of a wagon. A few irremovable boulders still remained;

but just when his services were most required,
Lieutenant Valcke, a Belgian engineer officer, arrived
on the scene, and promptly set to work to blast the
rocks. With his timely assistance the great work
was satisfactorily completed; and when the road
had been levelled with a deep layer of earth, the
way was open for the wagons to pass the point
which had threatened to bring their advance to an
abrupt conclusion.

Next a road was cleared across the wooded terrace,
and then a path was cut along the sides of a few
steep bluffs where it was necessary to level the
ground. This brought the expedition to a point
above the rapids where the Congo again became
navigable, and a good landing-place having been
found, a camp was formed, the wagons were unloaded, and the boats restored to their proper element.
Here, too, the party received an addition in the
arrival of Mr. Paul Neve, another young engineer,
who rendered valuable service in launching the *En
Avant*.

The Congo proved to be navigable to within three-
quarters of a mile of Isangila, and the last day of
1880 found the party at their destination. A landing-place was found in a cove—perhaps a trifle near
the cataract, but, with a little care, safely accessible; and there, on January 2, 1881, the boats
were beached, to be repaired and painted after their
nine months' knocking about. The road was fin-

ished, and with the comfortable assurance of "something attempted, something done," Stanley left Lieutenant Valcke and the other Europeans at Isangila, and once more went back to Vivi, where he found another reinforcement of Europeans, among them Captain Anderson, a Swedish merchant-sailor, who had brought a number of mules from Brussels.

Stanley's stay at Vivi was but short, and in the middle of February he was back at Isangila with two wagons, another steel lighter, and five hundred man-loads of materials. During his absence affairs had not been altogether prosperous; for his two principal assistants, Mr. Swinburne and Lieutenant Valcke, had both been ill, and on his return were still so feeble that it was necessary to send the former to Madeira, and the latter to Vivi, where he was to act as second in command.

Meanwhile Isangila camp had been fixed at a point above the cataract, and when the boats had been hauled up to it they were finally launched in readiness for a long voyage up-stream to Manyanga. Below was the wild, roaring cataract; on the farther shore a dreary cone of rust-coloured rock; all around silent hills and stony valleys, half hidden by tall grass. The outlook was weird and gloomy; but the place suited the practical work of the expedition, and the character of the scenery was a minor detail too unimportant for consideration. For the present, however, though a few men remained to keep open the line of communication, no station was founded at this somewhat dreary and forbidding spot.

Between February 23rd and May 1, 1881, the whole of the goods and material of the expedition were transferred from Isangila to Manyanga, where Stanley proposed to establish another trading-station. As, notwithstanding several rapids, the Congo was navigable all the way, this section of the journey was accomplished with comparative ease, though the steamers being unable to carry more than a small portion of the load at one time, it was necessary to make the journey in short stages, each of which had to be traversed several times. Sundry camps, therefore, were established by the way, and in connection with these two of the newly-arrived Europeans, Lieutenants Harou and Braconnier, made themselves specially useful, as their military knowledge rendered them well fitted to look after the details of camp life.

The journey was not wholly uneventful. On Sunday, February 27th, when, in accord with Stanley's custom, the expedition was enjoying a day of rest at Kilolo, a few miles above Isangila, shouts were heard, and shortly afterwards two missionaries appeared. They told an exciting tale of their adventures, for at one of the places they had visited the natives would have none of them, and for some time their lives seemed to be in imminent danger.

Finally the chief relented and allowed them to cross to the northern bank, where they met with a somewhat similar reception. Thoroughly alarmed, they then abandoned the idea of proceeding, and having obtained a canoe, descended the river in search of more friendly districts.

Two days after the departure of the missionaries Stanley sent some of his Zanzibaris to Vivi to carry a letter to the officer in charge, and also to bring up the European mail. Among the messengers was one Soudi, who, during Stanley's first journey down the Congo in 1877, had been swept over the Kalulu Falls and nearly drowned, and a little later had been captured and enslaved for a time by the natives. His various mishaps and adventures had not, however, sufficed to teach him wisdom, and when, some distance below Isangila, the party fell in with buffalo, he proceeded single-handed to stalk one of the herd. When sufficiently near he fired. The buffalo fell, and Soudi, casting caution to the winds, rushed in to cut the animal's throat. The buffalo, however, was not by any means disabled, and scrambling to his feet, he caught the luckless Soudi on his horns, tossed him high into the air, and mauled him so terribly that he died shortly after his companions came to the rescue. His death cast a gloom over the whole expedition, for he was a general favourite; but there was little time for grief, and the daily round of labour went on as before.

The pioneers had now reached a somewhat cheer-less region, where the Congo flowed between rugged hills, bare rocks, and barren soil, hardly relieved by occasional patches of dark green scrubby bush. Not a single village or hut broke the monotony; but on the hills, where the land was more fertile, were numerous villages, from which at intervals a fisher-man or two descended to the stream. Altogether the scene was anything but enlivening, and several of the members of the expedition, suffering perhaps from their depressing surroundings, became more or less seriously ill.

Much of the country around Manyanga was equally cheerless, though it was varied here and there by tree-clad ravines, and in some places, where the rocks formed what might be termed dry-land bays along the river bank, the soil washed down from above had formed fertile terraces. On one of these Stanley decided to land. There was a suitable harbour for the boats, a stream of clear, drinkable water—in fact, every convenience for a camp. The only draw-back was the fact that the terrace was cultivated, and might therefore command a high figure.

On April 29th the work of disembarkation was begun, and that afternoon two chiefs appeared from neighbouring villages with the customary offering of palm wine. Stanley hinted as delicately as he could that he wished to form a permanent settlement in the neighbourhood ; but somewhat to his discouragement, they did not seem to jump at the prospect, and all he could say only elicited permission to stay where he was for the present. Times had been bad, they said, of late ; all the other chiefs in the district had died, and the survivors seemed to feel a sort of vague, undefined mistrust of strangers. Still they were so far friendly that Stanley was able to hope for the best, and by the 1st of May the transfer of the goods from the last camp was completed.

Hard work, an unhealthy climate, or anxiety, or possibly a compound of all three, now proved too much for Stanley's strength, and scarcely was the new camp established when a slight feverish attack made itself felt. It was so trivial that he kept about as usual, until May 6th, when a fresh access of fever drove him unwillingly to bed. On the following day he was worse ; and although on May 10th he had his tent removed to the top of a hill nearly three hundred feet above the river, the fever continued to gain ground. Medicine seemed ineffectual ; but after a week of severe illness he took stronger measures, and swallowed twenty grains of quinine in a single dose. The first noticeable effect of this treatment was to render him partially unconscious ; but on recovering the power to think he was aware that, though he was extremely weak, the fever was less violent. Promptly following up the advantage gained, he took a second dose—this time of thirty grains of quinine. After this he once more lapsed

into unconsciousness, and for another six days lay
between life and death, with only occasional short
intervals of full consciousness. During all this time
he was tenderly nursed by his two young Africans,
Mabruki and Dualla; while Mr. Braconnier daily
visited him, to urge the necessity of taking nourish-
ment, and persevering in ever-increasing doses of
quinine.

Notwithstanding all their care, the invalid grew
steadily weaker. At last he became convinced that
he was dying, and on May 20th he sent Mabruki to
call up the other members of the expedition, in order
that he might bid them farewell. Dualla meanwhile
weighed out sixty grains of quinine, and when this
powerful dose had been dissolved in acid, and diluted
with a little Madeira to make it drinkable, Stanley
obediently swallowed the mixture. Its effects instantly made themselves felt; and when his companions, white and black, appeared on the scene,
for some minutes he struggled vainly to speak to
them. The words would not come, and all he could
do was to hold the hand of Albert Christopherson,
and endeavour to gain strength by gazing intently
into his eyes. Steadily the young fellow returned
the gaze; and then, possibly by some inexplicable
magnetism, strength returned to the sick man, and
he spoke clearly and intelligibly. With the power
of speech came also the conviction that he would
after all recover. " I am saved," he said; but in

his exceeding weakness the exertion had been too much, and as he spoke he fell back into unconsciousness, from which he did not awake for twenty-four hours. When he revived, his first desire was for something to eat—not for quinine. Of that he had had more than enough, and feebly calling Mabruki, he asked for some soup. Uncertain what to do, Mabruki consulted Braconnier, and the two compounded some broth, which the invalid drank with infinite satisfaction. From that hour he steadily improved, and by the end of the month was able to be up. On June 4th the arrival of the whaleboat, with the good news that a strong reinforcement from Zanzibar had reached Isangila, and that a young German named Lindner, with a specially-selected party, was hurrying up to Manyanga, gave him an additional fillip; for now, for the first time, he could venture to count on success.

Lindner, with twenty-four men, many of whom had served under Stanley on his previous journey, arrived on June 5th. He was full of life and energy —just the man for the work—and within a week he was off again to Isangila with the steamers to bring up the rest of the reinforcement.

Stanley, in the meantime, had gained strength so rapidly that the day after Lindner's departure he began to arrange for a pioneer journey to Stanley Pool. Before he could leave Manyanga, however, he had much to do. First, he must conclude his treaty

with the Manyanga chiefs; and then, when the necessary ground had been purchased, the actual work of
constructing the new station must be taken in hand.
There were tents to be cut out and made, a road to
be constructed, the station itself to be built, wagons
to be repaired, and a thousand and one incidental
duties to be performed. Each and all of these required his personal attention; and when he had put
Braconnier in charge of the road-makers, and detailed
Harou to superintend the building of the station,
he turned his hand to tent-making, wagon-repairing,
and an assortment of other handicrafts that might
well have dismayed a Jack-of-all-trades.

All this work occupied about a month, and during
that time Stanley had plenty of opportunity of ob-
serving native habits. Manyanga was evidently a
good site for a trading-station, for it was already
an important market centre, to which goods were
brought from all the country round. The chief
market, it appeared, was held about five miles from
the river; but every other day an exchange of
commodities took place on one or other of the hill-
tops around the new station. Traders bound from
the coast to Stanley Pool always made Manyanga
one of their halting-places, and thus the people had
grown accustomed to bring their produce thither for
sale. The only drawback was that they were apt
to be quarrelsome. Brawls were of frequent occurrence, and more than once Stanley's people be-

came involved, though he threatened them with dire consequences should any of them ever provoke a breach of the peace. On the whole, however, they behaved well, and not a single complaint was brought against them.

So long was the return of the boats delayed that Stanley became anxious. In the early part of July, however, the whaleboat appeared, and a letter from Lindner brought the news that, though all was well with his own party, the recently-arrived engineer, Neve, had died of fever at Isangila—the second white man who so far had fallen a victim to the climate.

CHAPTER IV.

NGALYEMA.

ON July 4th the reinforcement came up, and this time the news brought was good. All was going on well at Vivi; while at Isangila, Lieutenant Janssen, a new recruit from Belgium, was busily engaged in founding a station. Stanley's mind was thus set at rest; and having entrusted Lindner with the duty of bringing the goods and the main body of the expedition by water to Mpakambendi, he himself set out, with Messrs. Valcke and Braconnier and a few men, to travel overland to Stanley Pool.

For some time all went well. The country presented but few difficulties, the natives were friendly, and on July 26th the advance guard sighted Stanley Pool, without meeting with any special adventures. Another fourteen miles brought the party to the village of a chief named Bwabwa Njali, whose importance was mainly due to a ferry which at this point crossed a somewhat tumultuous tributary of the Congo. This chief was extremely friendly, though it was possible that his amiability partook

of the nature of cupboard love ; for while he refrained
from asking outright for presents, he expressed his
admiration of various objects in a manner which
left no room to doubt his desire to possess them.
From a native point of view he was a great dandy,
and most unusually clean in person. He was also
generous, and certainly set an example of liberality
in his gifts.

At this village Stanley received a visit from Malameen, a Senegalese non-commissioned officer, whom
the Comte de Brazza had left in charge of a strip
of territory purchased by him on behalf of France,
on the eastern bank of Bwabwa Njali's river. He
remained at the camp until the following day, when
Stanley went on to Mfwa, an ivory-trading village
situated on the north bank of the Congo, near the
spot where the river began to narrow below Stanley
Pool.

Here a most friendly reception was accorded to
the travellers, and a supply of food was promised ;
but in the morning the natives, instead of bringing
in meat and palm wine, delicately hinted that no
provisions were to be had. As there was no cultivated ground near the village, the statement seemed
to be unpleasantly true, and there was no course
open except to follow the advice of the chief and
move on to Malima, a large village some miles distant, on the northern bank of Stanley Pool.

Two hours' marching brought the advance guard

to this spot, where, in the chief Gamankono, Stanley recognized an old acquaintance, though he had evidently prospered since their last meeting. Each was pleased to see the other, and when Gamankono had seated himself on a huge crimson bolster, beneath which was spread a leopard skin, he proceeded to give a long account of everything that had happened since 1877. The pioneers were then conducted to a camping-place, and later in the day, when Gamankono and his sons paid another visit to Stanley, they expressed entire concurrence in his plan of founding a station at Malima.

But about sunset Malameen entered the village, and so poisoned the minds of the chief men against the newcomers, that during the night the crier proclaimed that no one was to have any dealings whatsoever with the strangers. That this was more than a mere threat soon became apparent, for in the morning a woman who had attempted disobediently to sell some fish was severely beaten by the other villagers, and some men made a threatening demonstration near the tents. Yet, on the other hand, Gamankono was apparently not ill-disposed, for three times he accepted Stanley's invitation to talk over matters, and three times offered an apology. He failed, however, to restore harmony; and seeing that, for the time being, at any rate, the case was hopeless, Stanley withdrew to Mfwa, where he proposed to open communication with Ngalyema, the chief of Kintamo, a village on the southern bank of the river.

Meanwhile, the evil reputation fastened on him by Malameen had preceded him to Mfwa. Before he reached that village the natives turned out in force to stop him, and a palaver ensued, in which he took occasion to point out their comparative weakness, and the very slight chance they would have should they attempt to try conclusions with him. This they clearly could not believe, and it seemed not impossible that the palaver would end in a fight; but before any actual breach of the peace had occurred, a number of strange natives raced up, shouting at the top of their voices for "Tanley." They came, it appeared, from Ngalyema, who had formerly made blood brotherhood with Stanley, and who now, being anxious to see him, had sent messengers across the river to guide the pioneers to a convenient camping-place near Mfwa.

This, so far as it went, was all very well; but now came the question of supplies. This was a serious matter, for the provisions brought from Bwabwa Njali's village were almost if not entirely consumed. No food was to be got in the neighbourhood, and while awaiting the promised interview with Ngalyema the column was face to face with famine. A whole day passed, however, and as no canoes appeared, three goats belonging to the expedition were killed, and, with a few small loaves, were distributed among the hungry men. Meanwhile, Stanley with his telescope eagerly watched the landing-place on the farther bank; but though plenty of canoes came and went, none made any attempt to cross the river.

On the morrow some messengers sent to purchase food from Bwabwa Njali were successful in obtaining one day's rations. Bwabwa Njali came back with the men, and on promising a further supply on the following day, received payment in advance in the shape of a roll of red cloth, much favoured in the neighbourhood. Later in the afternoon Ngalyema's nephew, a fine-looking young fellow, named Ganchu, appeared with a message from his uncle, who, it seemed, coveted a black Newfoundland dog named Flora, the property of one of the party. To offend the chief would have been impolitic, so Flora was given up and led off to her new master, who, however, had omitted to send any provisions.

In the morning men were sent to fetch up the supplies which Bwabwa Njali had promised; but to Stanley's dismay they returned empty-handed, with the news that Bwabwa Njali, instead of allowing them to cross the ferry, had threatened to shoot them, and had hinted that a general massacre might take place if the expedition did not at once leave the locality. Doubtless the unprincipled chief wished to retain the cloth he had received without performing his part of the bargain, and took this means of accomplishing his object.

Fortunately, Ngalyema came to the rescue, and was at once recognized by Stanley as his old acquaintance Itsi, who had prospered exceedingly, and now posed as the most important man in the district. He was accompanied by several minor chiefs, all of whom, possibly in imitation of their overlord, promptly clamoured to be admitted to blood brotherhood with various members of the expedition. To this desire willing assent was given. Did not present food and a future grant of land for a station depend on Ngalyema's good will? His opposition, as Stanley believed, would be little short of fatal to the success of the expedition; and consequently this expression of good will was cordially welcomed, and reciprocated with lavish gifts, including two donkeys, a looking-glass, a coat richly decked with gold lace, and a miscellaneous assortment of cloth, jewellery, and other articles of more or less value. In return for this liberality Ngalyema handed over to his " brother " his sceptre—a long brass-bound staff, which would convey assurance to all neighbouring chiefs that the bearer was the brother of Ngalyema, and must be treated with due respect. Scarcely was the ceremony completed, when Ingya, chief of Mfwa, appeared on the scene, and, ignoring all past unpleasantness, demanded to be admitted into Stanley's already large circle of brothers.

In the meantime Ngalyema had departed, taking with him Stanley's servant Dualla, for whose company he had made an urgent request. Four days later he returned, bringing Dualla with him, and demanded more cloth, and a large tin box which took his fancy. These were given to him, and he once more retired, promising to consult with the other chiefs on the matter of the land desired by Stanley.

Nearly a week passed, during which Stanley received an invitation to form a station at Kinshassa. In the circumstances no definite answer could be returned, and the pioneers waited until August 11th, when Ngalyema and five subordinate chiefs made their appearance. A long palaver followed; but still no definite answer could be obtained, as the natives, though perfectly friendly, were doubtful whether, from a commercial point of view, they would gain or lose by the presence of white men in their country. Finally the chiefs asked Stanley to allow ten of his best men to accompany them, while he, with the rest of his party, crossed the river and came up the south bank to Kintamo. As this was the greatest concession obtainable, Stanley supplied Susi—Dr. Livingstone's former companion—with a stock of goods and tools, and placed him in charge of the men who were to accompany Ngalyema. Lieutenant Valcke was then sent off to St. Paul de Loanda to purchase a fresh supply of trade goods, while the rest of the party returned to Mpakambendi, where Mr. Lindner had safely stored the goods left under his charge.

It was now considered desirable that a station
should be founded on the south bank of the Congo,
opposite Manyanga; and so well had Lindner ac-
quitted himself at Mpakambendi, that this duty
was assigned to him. He therefore departed on his
errand; and Stanley, while awaiting a reply from
the chiefs at Stanley Pool, occupied his men in
making roads and bridging some of the streams in
the neighbourhood of Mpakambendi. They were
thus employed until September 18th, when again
taking to the boats, they worked their way up the
Congo, and on October 11th landed on the south
bank near the confluence of the Lubamba River.
Thence for four days they travelled slowly and with
much trouble in the direction of Mtamo, until, at
the Ufuvu River, they were met by Susi and his
party.

Stanley then learned that Ngalyema's power was
not so great as he had been led to suppose. Instead
of being overlord of the whole district, he was
neither more nor less than an ivory trader who
owned a village and a good many armed slaves;
and when the neighbouring chiefs objected to the
suggested coming of the white men, he was power-
less to enforce his wishes. Evidently he had done
his best, but circumstances were against him, and
he was compelled to send Susi and his comrades
back to their master. With them also he returned
the two donkeys which had been given to him, and

directed the men to tell Stanley to found his station in Bwabwa Njali's country.

Amid all this disappointing news there was one spark of encouragement. This lay in Susi's discovery as to Ngalyema's real standing. If he would not receive the white men at his own village, it was now abundantly clear that he could not prevent them obtaining land in the neighbourhood, supposing that the Wambunda tribe, the real owners of the soil, made no objection. True, they did not seem very much disposed to welcome the expedition ; but as their prejudice was formed wholly on false reports of the evil disposition of the strangers, Stanley had little doubt that personal acquaintance would dispel their mistrust. Accordingly he gave orders for an advance, and the party travelled slowly through a well-populated district to the Iyumbi Mountain, on a spur of which a halt was made.

It now appeared that the most influential chief of the district was Makoko, whose territory lay on the Kintamo side of the mountain. Farther on a host of smaller villages were ruled by minor chiefs, all belonging to the Wambunda tribe. Makoko, at first misled by the unfavourable rumours, had been entirely averse to the coming of the whites, and had forbidden his people to trade with them. This had caused some inconvenience, as it became necessary to send men far and wide to obtain provisions ; though, on the other hand, the good conduct of the foragers became known over a wide area, and did much to remove unjust suspicions. The result was the removal of the ban. Free trading was sanctioned, and on November 7th, Makoko himself visited the camp with an imposing array of followers, many of whom were ivory traders who had been impelled by curiosity to join him.

Makoko was a pleasant-looking, little, old man, not over five feet in height, but boasting a wonderful beard, which he was compelled to curl, because when unrolled it measured six feet in length. He seated himself in state on a leopard skin, and when places for his followers had also been found, Stanley introduced himself as Bula Matari, formerly known in that region as Stanley, the first *mundele* who had been so far up the river. As a proof of the truth of his statement he produced Ngalyema's staff.

Makoko listened quietly, and when Stanley ceased speaking he replied that many stories of the wonderful doings of Bula Matari had reached his people. They had heard how he broke down rocks, cut roads through forests, and finally how he had made a treaty with Ngalyema. This angered them, for Ngalyema, being a stranger, whose village was a mere trading settlement, had no land to sell or give away, and so Makoko and his fellow-chiefs had stepped in to compel the white men to leave Kintamo. When, however, the expedition journeyed through Wambunda country, and nothing but good reports reached him, he knew that all was well. At the same time he would have the white men remember that the country south of the river belonged to him and his people, and that Ngalyema and the other traders had neither part nor lot in the matter. Stanley apologized for the mistakes he had made, by reason of his inability to distinguish men of one tribe from men of another, and then asked Makoko to grant him land near Kintamo on which to found a station. Makoko replied kindly granting the request. He was glad, he said, that white men should settle in his country, for he had often wished to see the wonderful people, who, as he was informed, made the cloth, guns, powder, glasses, and other goods brought up by the traders.

It was but natural that gratitude for the sudden removal of so many difficulties should open Stanley's heart, and inspire him to give large presents to Makoko, his wives, his children, and his followers. The chief was evidently gratified, and later that evening he came again to Stanley, and presented him with a sword as a sign to all men that they two were as brothers. All seemed well, and, full of hope and contentment, Stanley was about to go to bed when a messenger from Makoko came hurriedly to inform Bula Matari that Ngalyema with an armed force had arrived at Makoko's village, and was endeavouring to persuade the chief to join him in making war on the expedition. Makoko, however, had refused to go back on his word, and the messenger was to bid Stanley sleep in peace, as, if Ngalyema attacked him, Makoko and his men would assist Stanley.

For that night, at any rate, there was nothing to fear. Stanley, therefore, had time to think over matters, and evolve a plan which he had every hope would prove a success. Morning broke cloudy and wet, but about ten o'clock the sun came out. Calling his men together, Stanley instructed them to see that their pouches and cartridge belts were well filled, and then to take their guns and distribute themselves in their huts, in the boat or the wagon, in the tents and bushes—in fact, anywhere out of sight. Susi and his detachment, some of whom were known to Ngalyema, were to lounge idly about the camp; but no one, whether concealed or in the open, was to take any notice of whatever he might see or hear until the gong sounded. Then every man was to spring out, gun in hand, and rush about, shouting, waving his weapon—altogether conducting himself as much like a lunatic as possible.

" Do you understand ? " asked Stanley, when he had given his orders.

The men thoroughly appreciated the situation.

"*Inshallah*," they shouted, and dispersed to fetch their rifles and bestow themselves as their leader had directed. So quickly was everything done that a few minutes afterwards, when Ngalyema's force was

seen approaching, not a creature, except a few lazy-
looking Zanzibaris, was visible. Stanley himself sat
down to read, though his attention was so far detached from his book that he was able to note the
look of surprise with which the natives entered the
apparently deserted camp. Rising leisurely, he went
forward to meet Ngalyema, who made scant response
to his " brother's " effusive greetings, while Ganchu
and the other young chiefs wore a defiant, not to
say truculent aspect.

Ngalyema's first words were an inquiry as to why
his " brother " had come. To this question Stanley
replied by exhibiting the brass-bound staff, and
pointing out that he had acted in exact accordance
with Ngalyema's request that he would cross the
Congo, and approach Kintamo by land on the south
side of the river. At this point the sudden appearance of a party of Makoko's men caused Ngalyema
to change his tone, and confess that he was a stranger
living in the country for trading purposes only. He
had no objection, he added loftily, to trade with
white men ; but these particular members of the race,
in his opinion, had not come to trade, and must not
go to Kintamo. Stanley retorted that the land was
not Ngalyema's to give or withhold. Makoko was
going to give him land at Kintamo, on which he intended building a fine town, and Ngalyema could come
there and see him, or stay away, as pleased him best.

Finding that he was getting the worst of the

argument, Ngalyema took refuge in hinted threats,
to which Stanley calmly replied that he could reach
Kintamo that very day if he wished to do so. He
intended, however, to take his time, and advised
Ngalyema not to worry himself. Again Ngalyema
had got the worst of the argument, and unable,
apparently, to think of anything further to say, he
began a whispered consultation with some of his
attendant chiefs. Then changing his tone with
startling suddenness, he inquired what nice things
his "brother" had brought him from the coast.
Stanley's response was an invitation to his tent to
see for himself, and when piles of goods had been
brought out for inspection, the chief selected an
assortment which totalled up to something like £140
in value. These he graciously expressed his willingness to accept, on condition that the expedition
advanced no farther. To this proposition Stanley,
of course, could not consent, and finally Ngalyema
strode out of the tent in a rage; but standing for
a moment at the door he caught sight of the gong.
It at once aroused his curiosity, and forgetting his
displeasure he asked what it was.

"It is fetish," replied Stanley; but Enjeli, Ngalyema's son, ventured an assertion that it was some
kind of bell, whereupon the chief became possessed
with a desire to hear it. Stanley continued to assure
him that it was indeed fetish, which, if sounded, would
call up an armed force; it would be unwise to strike

it. Ngalyema insisted, and at last, with well-feigned reluctance, Stanley hit the gong. Its ringing tones resounded through the camp, and instantly, from tents, wagon, boat, and bushes, armed men appeared shouting and yelling and waving their guns. Faster and faster they streamed out, and Ngalyema's men, almost beside themselves with fear, dropped their weapons and fled incontinently. Ngalyema himself, too frightened to move, alone stood still, and Stanley, with becoming gravity, reminded him of their brother-hood. "Stand behind me, I will protect you," he said encouragingly.

Like a drowning man clinging to a straw the valiant Ngalyema jumped at the offer. While he clung to Stanley, Enjeli held tight to him, and the two dodged about in mortal fear, until, when their followers had all disappeared, Stanley thought the lesson had lasted long enough, and ordered his own men to fall into line. They obeyed instantly, and Stanley then suggested that he should strike the fetish again. But Ngalyema had had enough. He implored him not to touch the gong again, and it was not until the men had withdrawn that he at all recovered confidence. Enjeli and Ganchu then shouted to their men to come back, and the up-shot of the well-acted scene was that over a loving cup of palm wine, hastily fetched for the purpose, Ngalyema once more swore eternal friendship with his maltreated " brother."

CHAPTER V.

THE FOUNDING OF LEOPOLDVILLE.

BY the collapse of Ngalyema's opposition, all difficulties, except the material ones due to the nature of the country, were removed. Between Makoko's village and Kintamo sundry ridges, valleys, and streams intervened; but so many obstacles of this description had already been overcome, that these presented no terrors, especially as labour was now abundant. Apparently Ngalyema was not a favourite in the district, and no sooner was the little affair in which the "fetish" gong played so large a part noised abroad, than the Wambunda crowded to the camp to offer their services.

For carrying a load, weighing at least sixty pounds, to the neighbourhood of Kintamo—about sixteen miles distant—four red handkerchiefs were certainly not excessive payment. It was, however, considered satisfactory by the natives, and in one day seventy-eight porters were enlisted. The greater number of Stanley's own men were thus set free to devote their energies to road-making; and before the end of

November the expedition, with all its appurtenances, was safely in camp on the level ground near Kintamo.

Before setting to work to build, it now only remained to select a site. A hill, then called Khonzo Ikulu, a name afterwards changed to Leopold Hill, offered a breezy and commanding situation, which certainly was tempting ; but, then, it was some little distance from the landing-stage. Ngalyema's temper had been proved to be uncertain. He was now friendly ; but were he to change his mind, his men might easily swoop down and cut loose or destroy any boats that might be lying at anchor. The hill-top, therefore, clearly would not do.

After inspecting various possible sites, a spot on the slope of Leopold Hill was finally chosen. It was about eighty feet above the river, three hundred yards from the landing-place, and, further, commanded an extensive view both of Stanley Pool and also of the surrounding country. Altogether a better place could scarcely have been desired, and well pleased with his discovery Stanley returned to camp. Here he received a message from Ngalyema, who now wished to have the new station in his village ; but as arrangements had already been made with the Wambunda, Stanley could only politely decline the invitation.

Before building operations could begin it was necessary to level the ground, and this was accomplished by the excavation of a sort of terrace, around which a fence was constructed. There were also roads to be made ; timber to be cut and clay to be fetched for the station walls ; a garden to be cleared and planted ; sheds, storehouses, and quarters for the men to be built ; and a safe harbour to be constructed. All this work occupied about three months ; and when at length it was completed, the Europeans transferred themselves to comparatively palatial quarters in the blockhouse, which contained five private rooms, a dining-hall, and magazine, not to mention a grand array of shelves, where stores of all kinds—guns, cutlery, tools, crockery, glassware, drapery, jewellery ; everything, in fact, that an African native was likely to want—were displayed in tempting profusion.

While the work was in progress Ngalyema came out in his true colours. His original idea of the white man had evidently been of a being of unbounded wealth and liberality, of whom one had only to ask in order to have. On this point Susi had, it appeared, corrected him ; and his revised opinion that, though the white man might be rich, it was highly improbable that he would be content to give everything for nothing, was the cause of the change in his demeanour, and his refusal to allow a station to be founded at Kintamo. Then, when he learned that the white man was, after all, advancing, and that the Wambunda refused to oppose his progress, he once more altered his tactics. Possibly, after all, he might turn Stanley's coming to his own advantage; and in this hope he once more assumed a friendly air, and sent a variety of gifts to the camp, in the assurance that the foolish white man would reciprocate with something of far greater value.

Half a dozen times at least this hope was fulfilled, and then Stanley came to the conclusion that this sort of thing would not pay. Ngalyema had sent in goats, palm wine, bread, and ivory to the value of about £12, and for these had received over £100 worth of goods. Clearly a change must be made.

Consequently, on December 3rd, when Ngalyema appeared with his usual request for "something nice," a variety of fine things were shown him, and he was allowed, as usual, to select what he fancied. But instead of permitting him to carry off the goods Stanley laid his hand on them, and told him that before he could have any more presents he must promise to keep his people in order, and must also agree to a mutual law forbidding both his own and Stanley's men to go armed to each other's villages, lest quarrels should arise and fighting begin. This was a necessary precaution, as Makoko's men had reported that in Kintamo "everybody's finger was on the trigger," a concise statement which pointed to a very disturbed state of feeling.

Ngalyema promised that the new law should be duly promulgated in his village, and then departed with the goods he had chosen; but on the very next day he appeared at Leopoldville, as the new station was named, with a strong following of armed men. Stanley refused to admit them, and one of his men, in guarding the gate, was cut in the face by a spear. The injury was purely accidental, and when it was pointed out to Ngalyema, he professed the greatest concern. His sorrow, however, was only skin-deep, for on the following day he reappeared with another armed force, larger than before. This time he proposed to return the various gifts he had received, and break the brotherhood between himself and Bula Matari. Stanley replied that he could do as he pleased, and gave him to understand that the very next time his men came armed to the station it would be regarded as a declaration of war.

To this Ngalyema paid no sort of attention—possibly he considered himself strong enough to conquer any force that Bula Matari could put in the field; for the next afternoon (December 7th) Dualla informed Stanley that the chief, with about forty armed men, was approaching the camp, while another detachment, a hundred strong, was drawn up on the farther side of a small stream which flowed between the station and Ngalyema's village. Stanley thereupon armed a corresponding number of his own men, and marching out to meet Ngalyema, arranged them in skirmishing order near the path leading to Kintamo. Then, gun in hand, he advanced alone,

and asked sternly what Ngalyema meant. Was
there to be peace or war? At this show of force
Ngalyema instantly climbed down. Throwing away
his gun he grovelled before his "brother," making
such a humble appeal that Stanley, whose wrath
was only assumed, at once pardoned him; at the
same time improving the occasion by endeavouring
to impress on the chief that the station was simply
a market-place, to which guns must not be brought.
Ngalyema once more professed penitence. But his
protestations, as soon appeared, were empty words;
for no sooner was he safely back in his own village
than he sent messengers to his neighbours, asking
them to join him in making war upon Stanley.
One and all refused, and for some days Ngalyema
continued to sulk, wishing to attack, but not daring
to do so. Thus matters stood until two days before
Christmas, when Kondo, a neighbouring chief, undertook to make peace, and on Christmas Eve a grand
palaver was held.

All the principal chiefs of the neighbourhood were
present, and when all had assembled Ngalyema was
formally accused of endeavouring to sell land belonging to the Wambunda. Bula Matari was then
called upon to relate his side of the story, which
showed that, in his original dealings with Ngalyema,
there had been no question of land transference, and
that his gifts to the chief had been merely in recog-
nition of a supply of food sent to him. Then at a

sign from Stanley, Dualla gave Ngalyema the recognized token of acquittal by drawing a pipe-clay line from Ngalyema's wrists to his shoulders—a native custom which Koko, in his desire for peace, had secretly confided to Stanley. Finally, the meeting broke up in the greatest good-humour, and many pounds of powder were expended in firing guns to celebrate the event.

Towards the end of March 1882, a caravan from Manyanga brought news that Flamini, the Italian engineer of the *Royal*, had been invalided home on account of an accident which had befallen him. Further, a reinforcement of seventy-eight coloured men, who had left Isangila on February 19th, were still somewhere on the road, as the European in charge had deserted his post and left his men to look after themselves. There was nothing for it but to send a detachment to bring them in, and on the 8th of April they arrived in safety.

By way of consolidating the peaceful relations, Stanley and Ngalyema entered into renewed blood brotherhood. The two crossed arms, a slight cut was made in each arm, salt was sprinkled over the incisions, which then were rubbed together, while a fetish man on Ngalyema's side, and Susi on Stanley's, called down the dire vengeance of the gods on either of the two who should break the brotherhood thus established.

The prospects of the expedition now looked highly

encouraging. Not only had stations been built and roads made, but a lively trade began to spring up. Every five days caravans passed backwards and forwards between Manyanga and Leopoldville, while from all the country round natives came in with produce for sale. Much more, indeed, was brought in than could be purchased; and as everything was now in smooth running order, Stanley, who was emphatically a pioneer, not a trader, became anxious to go forward. He was, indeed, only remaining at Leopoldville till the arrival of the officer who was to take charge of the station.

CHAPTER VI.

DISCOVERY OF LAKE LEOPOLD.

THE long-expected officer at length made his appearance, and on April 19th Stanley, with Lieutenant Janssen, Albert Christopherson, another European, and about fifty coloured men, including Stanley's old companions, Uledi and Susi, embarked in the *En Avant*, the whaleboat, and two canoes, to seek a convenient site for another station. It was the first time a steamer had ever plied on the waters of Stanley Pool; and for a time the little craft, with the two canoes in tow, hugged the southern shore. So strong was the current that it was all she could do to hold her own; but yard by yard she crept along, until, on reaching the village of Kinshassa, she cast off the tow rope, and leaving the canoes, struck boldly across the channel to Bamu Island in the centre of the Pool. The island was a long, low-lying piece of ground, the greater part of which showed unmistakable signs of being flooded whenever the stream was high; but it was well covered with grass and timber, and appeared to be the home of numerous wild animals, especially hippos, to whose amphibious nature the place was, no doubt, specially suited.

After skirting the shore of the island for some hours, a camping-place was found, and the crews landed for the night. A supply of wood for fuel was cut; but shortly after midnight a heavy storm came down, and so soaked the wood that in the morning, though the rain had cleared off, it was no easy matter to get up steam. When this was at last accomplished, the *En Avant*, once more taking the boats in tow, proceeded on her way up the Pool. Many were the miseries of the voyage, for the steamer was filled to overflowing with boxes and bales, and on these the pioneers had to crouch, exposed to the terrific heat of the sun, while the neighbourhood of the boiler added greatly to their suffering. But slow as the progress was, at last the end of the Pool was reached, and the boats emerged into the upper reaches of the Congo. Unfortunately, by this time a sense of physical discomfort had mastered most other feelings, and no one had thoughts to spare for the magnificent scenery of the great river, though Stanley, who had travelled in many countries, and seen some of the most celebrated rivers of the world, was afterwards fain to confess that none of them approached the glory of the Congo. At the time, however, cramped, half broiled, and wholly uncomfortable, he had no eyes for scenery, and was unfeignedly glad when, on April 26th, the boats were anchored at Mswata, a village on the south bank of the stream. The position seemed favourable for a station, and an invitation to land was willingly accepted.

The chief, a stout and very ordinary-looking personage, named Gobila, made no secret of his real position. He was no territorial ruler, but a well-to-do ivory trader, who, by permission of Gandelay, chief of the Banfunu tribe, had built a village as a centre for his trading operations. He made no pretence of being a chief in his own right, with power over the land, and when Stanley asked him to grant a site for a station he frankly said that he had no power to do so.

News of the arrival of the white men speedily reached Gandelay, and he came in state, with three canoes, a band of drums, horns, and bells, several attendants to brush off the flies, a hammock in which he was carried, and other paraphernalia, to greet the new arrivals, to whom he presented the usual gifts. Gobila then introduced the subject on which he desired to have Gandelay's opinion. Bula Matari, he said, wished to found a settlement in the neighbourhood, and he was willing to have the white man for a neighbour. But being there himself only, so to speak, on sufferance, as a trader, he had no right to make a grant of land, though, so far as his power went, he was willing to offer a choice of sites near his own village, if Gandelay would authorize him to do so.

No sooner had he finished speaking than Ganchu, the Bateke chief who owned the land on the farther bank, declared his willingness—nay, more, his desire —that the white man should settle in the country. If Gandelay would not have him, he had only to cross the river to find a warm welcome, and all the land he wanted, as well as plenty of trade. Then it was Gandelay's turn to speak. He was, he said, supreme chief of all that region, but the land in that particular locality he had given to Gobila. He might do as he would, and if he accepted the white man the Banfunu would do likewise, and Bula Matari should be the brother of Gandelay.

Nothing could have been more satisfactory, and when a site had been selected, Lieutenant Janssen, who was to take charge of the new station, was told off to superintend its erection. Stanley meanwhile paid a flying visit to Leopoldville, where he received an enthusiastic welcome. He had, however, no time to linger, and on May 14th was back at Mswata. Here matters were progressing in a most satisfactory way, and Lieutenant Janssen had established himself in Gobila's good graces. There was no need for Stanley to remain at Mswata; but as, until more Europeans came up, he could not go farther afield, he determined to use the time of waiting in exploring the Kwa River.

This stream, he learned, was formed by the union
of two rivers—one, the Mbihi, of white water; the
other, called the Mfini, a black stream. The Mbihi,
if accounts were to be believed, was altogether a
most remarkable river; for it was said to be subject
to some sort of explosions, during which the water
suddenly rose up in fury, raged for a while, and then
abruptly sank to its normal calmness. The black
Mfini, on the other hand, was a broad river, navigable
from its mouth to a point many miles distant, where,
according to the natives, the two banks curved round
and met—a phenomenon which Stanley supposed to
be really a *sudd*, or barrier of tangled water-plants,
such as obstructs some parts of the Nile.

The proposed trip was expected to occupy about
nine days, so provisions and trade goods sufficient
for that period were placed on board the *En Avant ;*
and Stanley, with Christopherson, who acted as
engineer, a coloured crew, and a couple of native
guides, set out. Less than four hours' steaming
brought them to the mouth of the Kwa, which
proved to be a broad, rapid, winding stream, considerably darker in colour than the Congo. Two
or three uninviting-looking villages were passed, and
it was not until after sunset that a suitable camping-
place was found, near a village ruled by one of
Gobila's brothers. The place had rather a poverty-
stricken air, but a kindly welcome was accorded to
the travellers; and in the morning, while the crew

turned out to cut firewood, Stanley was taken by
one of the guides to see the fields of cassava, sugar-
cane, and ground-nuts. These productions he was
allowed to sample to his heart's content, and was
permitted, further, to take back a supply to Christopherson, who was engaged in getting up steam.
Soon all were once more on board, and the little
steamer puffed noisily off towards Musye, where
Gankabi, a rather celebrated person in those parts,
was queen.

The next afternoon Musye was reached. It was
a large, straggling, and eminently prosperous-looking
place, with a capital position for trade, as it faced
the confluence of the Mfini and the Mbihi, and had,
of course, convenient access to the Congo. Crowds
of people turned out to gaze at the wonderful boat
which, of its own power, could travel up-stream,
and to welcome the scarcely less wonderful white-
faced visitors. Gankabi, however, was not at home,
and her subjects did not know when she would
return. In her absence no one ventured to invite
the travellers to land; and even Eela, the wife of a
trader, who had made acquaintance with Stanley at
Mfwa, where she had been extremely friendly, now
declined to have anything to do with him. There
was no choice but to go ahead, and the *En Avant*,
with her attendant boats, pushed on to a conveniently
situated island some miles farther up the Mfini.
Here the explorers camped, but soon discovered

that they had not by any means chosen an ideal resting-place, for scarcely had they settled down when they were attacked by swarms of mosquitoes. Out from the tall grass they came in clouds; and though a circle of fires was lighted, in the hope that the smoke would be some protection, not one whit did the insects care, and the hapless crew passed a miserable night.

In the morning came the usual search for firewood —a rare article in that locality, where spear grass was the principal product. This grass had its uses, for an inferior kind of salt largely used by the natives was obtained from its ashes.

About an hour after the boats got under way two large canoes were seen approaching, and seated in one of them was a fine-looking woman, whom the guides soon recognized as Gankabi. Both parties came to a standstill, and Gankabi, in the style of one accustomed to obedience, commanded Stanley to go back with her. This he politely declined to do; and when she insisted, he pointed out that, great as Gankabi might be, he was Bula Matari, the man who broke rocks and rose superior to all difficulties.

Of course the inference intended was that he was the greater of the two; but Gankabi failed to see the force of the argument. Finally a compromise was effected by Stanley consenting to accompany her to a neighbouring village, where she obtained for him a goat and some bananas. At this place she wished

him to wait, while she went up to another large
settlement, called Ngete; but fearing complications,
and having no mind for further argument, after
waiting for a little time, he decided to go on his
way. On approaching Ngete a full head of steam
was got up, and the boat dashed past in fine style;
while Gankabi, standing on the bank, helplessly
watched the white man's disregard of orders.

Several villages were passed, and on May 26th the
boat came to a point where two streams met. Stanley
decided to pursue his course up the right-hand stream
—the broader of the two—and he soon became aware
that the current was less strong than before. Then
the channel widened out, and he grew more and
more convinced that he was approaching a lake, of
whose existence hitherto not so much as a rumour
had reached Europe. The water was very dark in
colour, and at that point was covered with sulphur-
coloured dust, which, in the rays of the westering
sun, glittered like cloth of gold. It was, however,
time to think of halting for the night, and the camp
was pitched on a smooth pebbly beach, backed by
a line of dark impenetrable-looking forest. Here
plenty of good hard firewood was obtainable, and
the remaining daylight was spent in laying in a
stock for use on the following day.

In the morning the *En Avant* steamed merrily
forward into what soon proved to be a new lake of
considerable size, since to the eastward, far as the

eye could reach, nothing but water was visible. This was a discovery well worth making; and, fired with new zeal, Stanley pushed rapidly ahead, regardless of the fact that the contemplated nine days were already ended, and that provisions were rapidly lessening.

The day passed without incident. No sign of human life was seen, and the explorers began to think that, save for the birds and beasts, they had the lake to themselves. On the following morning, however, on rounding a point they came suddenly on a small fleet of fishing canoes, and saw in the distance the village to which the boats doubtless belonged. At first the fishermen were too much absorbed to notice the approach of the strange, snorting object which was so rapidly bearing down upon them; but when at last they perceived it, their horror was extreme. What on earth could it be ? For a few moments they gazed in silent wonderment, and then it occurred to one of them to seek safety in flight. As his paddles struck the water, the others recovered from their first alarm, and soon all but one were rapidly skimming off in the direction of home. He, poor fellow, was much farther from land, and so far had remained unconscious of the new and unheard-of terror that had invaded his peaceful waters.

Suddenly he turned round, and catching sight of the boat with sail spread and paddles revolving, he

sank down in his canoe in abject fear. Then, as the
steamer approached, he pulled himself together, cast
a despairing glance around, and began to paddle for
dear life, dodging skilfully as the steamer pursued
him. In this way he gained a little time; but by
degrees the *En Avant* overhauled the canoe, and
realizing that he could not escape by paddling, as
a last resource he sprang overboard and disappeared
from view.

Slowly the steamer moved towards the empty
canoe, and at a word from Stanley, Dualla and Uledi
held themselves ready to jump overboard and catch
the frightened fisherman. As the object of his fears
approached he dived in terror; but the Zanzibaris
were too quick for him. Over they went, and
in a few moments swam back with their captive,
who was quickly taken on board, where the two
guides spoke soothingly to him in the hope of gaining his confidence. At first no answer was forthcoming, and then it appeared that the poor fellow
thought his captors intended to make a slave of
him. He could or would give no information; and
it was not until he had been laden with gifts and
allowed to paddle off, that he realized that no evil
was intended, and that he was a rich man, free to
do what he would.

By May 31st, Lake Leopold II., as Stanley named
his new discovery, had been successfully circum-
navigated and explored. It covered a considerable

area, probably as much as eight hundred square miles; but it was everywhere shallow, though, in addition to a large tributary which entered its northern end, it was fed by numerous small streams. From a few words spoken by the captured fisherman, it appeared that slave hunters had been busy in the locality; and this doubtless accounted for the extreme shyness of the natives, none of whom would so much as approach the explorers, though the guides said that they did a large trade with Gankabi in rubber, fish, redwood, ivory, and powder. The immediate result of their shyness was that no supplies had been obtainable, and consequently, as the provisions on board were exhausted, by the time the boats reached Gankabi's village the crews were in a ravenous condition; while, to make matters worse, Stanley found himself in the grip of a severe attack of fever. Three days' halt did not benefit him. He grew worse rather than better, and was compelled to resign the command to Christopherson, who safely navigated the boat to Leopoldville.

For nearly three weeks Stanley remained in a semi-conscious state, varied by occasional intervals during which he was able to think clearly. In one of these it occurred to him that the three years for which some of the Zanzibaris had been engaged were at an end; they had a right to their discharge, and he gave directions that they should convey him as far as Vivi on their way to the coast. Of the events of the journey he had little knowledge, for it was not until Mpakambendi was reached that he permanently regained anything like full consciousness. He was still very ill; indeed, fresh disorders manifested themselves, and he was heartily glad of a few days' rest at Isangila, where Mr. Swinburne had contrived to impart quite a homelike aspect to his surroundings.

At Vivi, where the party arrived on July 8th, less progress had been made. The garden, indeed, had prospered finely, but the bridges and roads were out of repair, and only one magazine had been added to the original structures. It was disappointing; but a surprise awaited Stanley, which in some degree turned his thoughts from vexatious subjects.

Among the Europeans who came out to greet him was Dr. Peschuel Loeche, who had done good service as an explorer in West Africa, and who, as Stanley had been informed some months previously, had been entrusted by the Committee with some important work in the Loango district. What was Stanley's surprise, then, when a man whom he had fully believed to be far away in the interior welcomed him at Vivi. Weak, ill, and unfit for work as he was, it was a great relief to his mind when Loeche showed him a sealed commission from the President of the Congo Association, by which, in the event of Stanley's becoming incapacitated by illness or accident, the doctor was empowered to act for him.

A holiday was the very thing he needed, and when the time-expired Zanzibaris had been started on their homeward voyage under the charge of Christopherson, whose service was also at an end, Stanley set out for Europe.

On the way several delays occurred, and it was not until October that he appeared before the Committee of the Congo International Association, into which the "Committee of Study" had expanded, to report progress. More had been done than had originally been planned: five stations had been founded instead of the three contemplated; a steamer and a sailing boat instead of a single steamer had been launched on the Upper Congo; while roads and bridges, about which no special stipulations were made, had been constructed. Further, the natives along the route were all amiably disposed and quite ready to trade. Altogether, the Committee had good reason to be satisfied; but if the work already accomplished was to bear permanent fruit, much still remained to be done. Of this fact the members expressed themselves as thoroughly convinced, and if only Stanley would continue at the head of affairs they were quite prepared to go forward. To this, in his broken health, he was disposed to demur, but he finally consented to return to Africa on condition that the Committee provided him with an efficient second in command, who should take charge on the Lower Congo while he was engaged

on the Upper Congo.   To this very reasonable request
ready consent was given, and when Stanley suggested
General Gordon as a suitable man King Leopold
promised to endeavour to obtain his services.   On
this understanding Stanley agreed to limit his holiday
to six weeks, and then to resume work on the Congo,
where the territory acquired by purchase and treaty
was rapidly assuming the dimensions of a state.

CHAPTER VII.

IN HARNESS AGAIN.

BY the middle of December 1882, Stanley, refreshed and strengthened by his run to Europe, was once more at Vivi. But while he was gaining vigour everything on the Congo seemed to have gone wrong. Dr. Peschuel Loeche, of whom so much had been expected, had suddenly forsaken his charge and gone home. The chief officers of Vivi and Isangila, and the second in command at Leopoldville, had likewise taken their departure. The chief of Leopoldville had given himself a holiday and gone to the coast, and the *En Avant* had had her steam valve stolen.

Stanley's first care was to restore order at Vivi, the station on which all the others depended for their supplies. The captains of the steamers—by way, probably, of saving themselves trouble—had taken to discharging their cargoes anywhere but at the proper place, and leaving to the station staff the work of conveying the goods to their destination. Much unnecessary labour was thus entailed, for the cargoes were frequently put ashore more than a mile below the landing-place. At first sight the matter seemed one that might easily be rectified; but sundry complications had arisen, which induced the captains to resent interference from Stanley, and it was not without trouble that he carried his point.

Having settled this matter, he turned his attention to the equipment of an expedition under the command of Captain Elliot, who was commissioned to found a line of stations to connect Isangila with the Kuilo River, a stream entering the sea some distance north of the Congo mouth. The intervening country was somewhat difficult; but as the formation of the stations would open up a rich trading district hitherto unexplored, it was most desirable that the work should be accomplished. A few days later, therefore, as the difficulties promised to be even greater than was expected, Stanley detached a young lieutenant named Van de Velde from his post at Vivi, and sent him round by sea with an auxiliary force to the Kuilo mouth. A better man for the work could not have been found, for in a surprisingly short time Van de Velde took over the establishment of a trader named Saboga, and converted it into a new station, which he named Rudolfstadt. Not content with this, he proceeded up-stream, making treaties as he went with the chiefs, and establishing friendly relations with all the natives from the Kuilo mouth to the rapids, twenty-eight miles from the coast.

He was a most valuable officer; but his health would not stand the climate, and after a few months at Vivi, whither he returned on the arrival of Captain Elliot at Rudolfstadt, he was compelled to resign his commission.

Stanley, in the meantime, had settled a dispute with the Vivi natives, whose righteous indignation had been aroused by a French employé of the association. This man, in a moment of anger at some trifling annoyance, had whipped out his revolver and fired at Massala, the native linguist who had done such good service at the time when the station was founded. The wound, fortunately, was not mortal, but the natives were extremely angry; they swarmed down on the station to demand vengeance, and were only appeased when, the offender having been duly tried, Stanley requested the chiefs to pronounce sentence. They retired to consider the penalty, and on their return said they would be satisfied with the payment of a fine amounting in value to over £400. The amount seemed excessive, but by Stanley's intervention a compromise was effected, and the fine reduced to the more reasonable value of £24, 4s. To this was to be added the offending revolver, which was condemned to be smashed, while its owner further was banished for ever from Vivi territory.

Again journeying up the river, Stanley arrived on February 4th at Manyanga, whence he dispatched

Captain Hanssens to open up another section of country between that station and the Upper Kuilo district. At the same time, Lieutenant Valcke was requested to travel along the south bank of the Congo, and make treaties with the chiefs through whose territories he passed. Various other officers were detailed to perform sundry services, ranging from treaty-making to boat-building—one and all, whatever their apparent importance, stones in the edifice which Stanley had undertaken to construct.

On nearing Leopoldville a letter from the commandant, who had been summarily ordered back to his duties, informed Stanley that the station staff was almost at starvation point, and totally unable to feed a large influx of visitors. Such a state of affairs seemed utterly incomprehensible, and Stanley, having sent forward what provisions he could spare, made the best of his way onward. Progress, however, was slow ; for the rains had damaged the road, and the wagon, heavily laden with the steam launch *Royal*, frequently broke down. But perseverance conquered difficulties, and mile after mile was left behind. As the travellers neared the Pool, the natives crowded round with friendly greetings and gifts of provisions. Their evident pleasure at Stanley's return made the reports from Leopoldville the more puzzling, for, according to them, not a native would go near the station. How was such conflicting evidence to be reconciled ?

The first sight of the station was another disappointment. Stanley had been picturing it to himself as improved in every respect; but instead of the flourishing gardens and fruit trees he had expected, he beheld a grass-grown wilderness, in which the roofs of the men's huts were barely visible. The blockhouse had an almost equally uncared-for appearance; the treasury was almost empty; the trees were conspicuously absent; and the steamer and whaleboat lay neglected and weather-worn at the little wharf.

After mastering as many details as possible, and accepting the resignation of the obviously incapable chief officer, who was forthwith sent down to the coast, Stanley summoned the neighbouring chiefs to a palaver, in the hope of coming to a more satisfactory state of affairs. First, Ngalyema stated his grievances : he had been improperly treated, he considered, by some of the officers, who had spoken rudely to him and threatened him ; while as for the chief of the station, just departed, it was impossible to get on with him. Consequently, Ngalyema had thought it best to give the station a wide berth.

One of the offending officers then told his side of the story. According to his account, Ngalyema had exaggerated everything, and had acted in a quarrelsome and aggravating manner. He himself had possibly been unduly rough ; but if so, that was

the worst fault he had committed, and if blamed
he was quite ready to resign.

Thus each party accused the other of causing the
trouble, and Stanley had to judge as best he could
between them. Both, he remarked, seemed to have
been in the wrong, but Ngalyema should have known
better than to take offence as he had done. Most
of the officers with whom he had quarrelled should
be transferred to other stations ; but with one, named
by the natives Tembo, or the Elephant, whom he
had previously misjudged, he must make peace.

Tranquillity was thus restored, and the station
began to assume a more prosperous air. The grass
was cut ; the men's dwellings were removed to a
better situation, while their original site was converted into a plantation of bananas, mangoes, and
papaws. The terrace was enlarged, its slopes faced,
and a variety of other improvements were made.
Best of all in Stanley's eyes was the triumph over
native prejudice, which he felt was assured when the
terrace became accepted as a regular market-place,
to which day after day women and children from
all the country round brought goods for sale.

The boat-builders were also busy at this time.
The *Royal* and *En Avant* had been thoroughly overhauled, and a new steam launch, named the *A. I. A.*
(Association Internationale Africaine), had been built
and launched. With these three, the whaleboat, a
canoe, and eighty men, Stanley proposed to explore

the Upper Congo, and on May 9th the flotilla set sail. That night the party halted at Kimpoko, a new station in process of construction near the head of Stanley Pool, and two days later dropped anchor at Mswata, where a few days were passed pleasantly, while fresh stores of provisions for the journey were procured. On the 15th the expedition was once more afloat; and late that day, on nearing Bolobo, where Captain Hanssens had established a station, Stanley was met by messengers bearing a letter from the officer in charge, who, unfortunately, had no good news to tell. Troublous times, it seemed, had begun, and two of the men attached to the station had been murdered.

Further details were forthcoming on the following day, when the expedition reached Bolobo. For some months all had gone well. Lieutenant Orban, the first commandant, had the knack of getting on with the natives, and during his reign peace and harmony prevailed. But the loneliness of the life was unendurable. He applied for leave, and his successor failed to agree with his black neighbours. He, in his turn, was relieved by another officer, who likewise was unable to preserve friendly relations.

The position was no doubt a difficult one, inasmuch as there was jealousy of long standing between Ibaka, the chief of Bolobo, and his neighbours. The affair had been patched up and peace restored; but when the white men formed a station at Bolobo, the other chiefs were pleased to regard their coming as an undue accession of strength for Ibaka. Their jealousy flamed up afresh, and their hatred was extended to the unoffending whites, whose people only passed their own boundaries at the risk of severe maltreatment if caught by their truculent neighbours. This state of affairs went on for some time, and culminated in the murder of the two men, who, having ventured to cut wood near the hut of a chief named Gatula, had been foully slain. On the following morning one of Gatula's men climbed a tree close to the station boundary, and from this vantage ground challenged one, Sergeant Khamis, to fight. Khamis accepted the challenge, and going out with his rifle shot the aggressor dead.

Matters had reached this stage when Stanley appeared on the scene. News of his arrival quickly reached Ibaka, who, with his headman Lugumbila, came down to the station to consult with Bula Matari as to the measures to be taken. Was it to be war or peace ? There could be no question but that Gatula deserved punishment, and, still less, that Stanley was in a position to inflict it, should he see fit to do so. But if he fought here at Bolobo, who could tell what adverse rumours might precede him up the river ? Ill-advised action at this stage might imperil the whole future of the expedition ; yet to leave the murder unavenged would be considered tantamount to a confession of weakness. On these grounds Stanley decided to demand a fine. He would wait, he said, two days, and then, if payment was not forthcoming, he would force Gatula to submit.

On the second day a palaver was held by the chiefs; but a thunderstorm broke up the meeting before anything was settled, and the next day Stanley was informed that Gatula had fortified his village. This looked like a preparation for hostilities; but a renewal of the conference brought the recalcitrant chief to a better frame of mind, and he consented to pay the fees for the administration of justice which native law allowed to the two chief judges, Bula Matari and Ibaka. This fee, in Stanley's case, consisted of a goat, five fowls, a quantity of camwood powder, some palm oil, two bunches of bananas, in addition to which the restoration of a rifle belonging to one of the murdered men was demanded.

Payment of the legal fees having been duly made, the fine or blood-money was fixed at three thousand brass rods, the cash value of which was £50. Evidently this was more than Gatula had bargained for. He offered a tusk of ivory weighing fifty-eight pounds. This, at the price at which ivory had been sold to the expedition by the Bateke traders at Stanley Pool, was worth less than £10, and was consequently at once refused. Gatula was informed that he must pay the sum demanded, and the matter was finally compromised by the handing over of brass rods to the value of £42, 4s., which Stanley consented to accept in full settlement.

Matters being thus satisfactorily arranged, Stanley was at liberty to continue his journey up the Congo, whose banks were now in many places clothed with dense forest. The character of the river itself had also changed, and from a roaring torrent closely shut in by rocky cliffs it had become a broad, tranquil river, thickly studded with islands, some of them several miles in length. Still, however, the current was strong enough to retard the progress of the steamers; and, heavily burdened as they were, they seldom made more than two and a half knots per hour, and from twenty to thirty miles a day was the average distance covered.

About five o'clock in the evening the boats were generally moored for the night, and the crews went ashore to cut wood for the next day's consumption, while the cooks prepared supper. For an hour and a half all hands were engaged in hunting up the driest wood to be found in the neighbourhood, and hauling it to the camp before daylight failed. Then by the light of a huge fire the wood-cutters fell to, and chopped and sawed the logs into suitable lengths; while the white men, absolved from further labour, sat down to their evening meal. Thus every day was very much like the day that went before it; while, to add to the monotony of life, the bill of fare admitted of few variations. Some sort of vegetable soup, cassava bread, fowls, goat meat, desiccated potatoes, and rice were the bulk of the eatables commonly available, though occasionally sweet potatoes, yams, or bananas made an agreeable variety. " Early to bed," with a view to " early to rise," was the rule; and thus, as day followed day in monotonous sameness, it was perhaps excusable if, as time went on, every member of the party craved for some little variety in the daily round.

After several days, with little or no intercourse with the natives, provisions began to run short. A break in the forest, with what appeared to be a considerable settlement, was therefore a welcome sight. Speed was slackened, and as the steamers slowly passed in front of the huts, whose inmates had flocked to the river bank to behold the wondrous sight, all sorts of tempting goods—coloured cloths, bright handkerchiefs, brass rods, gaudy beads—were displayed in tempting profusion. Meanwhile one of the men who hailed from Mswata shouted out the praises of Bula Matari in a stentorian voice; but still no halt was made. Thus one village was passed, then a second, and at the third a reply was shouted back to the effect that the chief was dead, and that those of the inhabitants who had not died of smallpox were in course of dying from starvation. Proper sympathy was expressed; but as the " famishing people " looked remarkably fat and well, the statement of their evil case was taken for what it was worth, and passing on a little farther the expedition halted as usual for the night.

The ruse succeeded admirably. Very soon up came the natives laden with bananas, fowls, goats, plantains, and a variety of other edibles, for sale. So plentiful was the supply that in an hour or two several days' provisions for the whole expedition had been purchased, and at sunrise on the following morning a further assortment was forthcoming. These too were gladly bought up, and the natives were gently rallied on their remarkable statements of the previous day with regard to the famine and smallpox which they had declared were raging in the village. Then, with a promise to return later on, since the locality seemed a favourable one for the foundation of a station, the pioneers bade their new acquaintances good-bye, and the wearisome voyage was resumed.

Ngombe, a rich and populous district, where the rearing of crocodiles for sale was found to be a profitable industry, was passed on June 4th. Here the river occupied a comparatively narrow channel not more than two miles wide, where the current was proportionately strong, inasmuch as here was gathered together all the water which, both above and below the narrows, spread itself over a bed from four to six miles wide. The steamers, however, safely negotiated the passage, and later in the day arrived off Usindi, where the inhabitants were

so anxious to trade that they fairly took the expe
dition by storm in their eagerness to welcome the
strangers. Nothing was too good for them. It wa
a case of "ask and have," if only they would stay
and build. So anxious, indeed, were the native
to avoid giving offence and causing alarm, tha
every warlike weapon was scrupulously kept out o
sight. There was nothing but friendliness and goo
will.

Irebu, some miles higher up the stream, wa
another important trading district, whose powerfu
tribes had overawed the whole region. At the tim
of Stanley's visit they were at war among themselves
and Stanley, having made blood brotherhood wit
one of the chiefs named Mangombo, was called upo
to make peace. The cause of the dispute was rathe
complicated. Some time previously, while on
trading excursion, the Irebu men—some of whom
belonged to Mangombo's village of Upper Irebu, an
some to that of Magwala, chief of Lower Irebu—fe
out with the Bangala tribes. Though the Irebu me
managed to save their ivory, they fared badly in th
fight, for thirty-three of their number were killed
of whom twenty-eight belonged to Mangombo'
village. Trade, of course, came to a standstill; bu
after a while Mpika, chief of Central Irebu, made
descent on some Bangala trading canoes, and cap
tured eight men. As Mangombo's men had suffere
so severely in the original fight, he considered tha

the larger number of Mpika's captives should have been handed over to him. Mpika could not see the force of the argument. He refused to hand over any of his captives; and as Magwala backed him up in his decision, Mangombo appealed to arms. So far the result had been unsatisfactory in the extreme: trade was stopped; more lives had been lost; except at night, no one dared to go out; and in all the villages of Irebu there were lamentation, mourning, and woe. Could not Bula Matari, of whom so much had been heard, do anything to restore peace and good will?

Stanley replied that he would gladly act as peacemaker, but that just then his time was precious. Let them stop fighting until his return down-stream, and then he would see what he could do. The idea of a truce, with the prospect of future peace, pleased Mangombo well; but would the other chiefs agree? This was his only doubt; and when Stanley went in his boat to make overtures to them, he found Magwala by no means easy to deal with. Mpika, however, having made blood brotherhood with Lieutenant Janssen, was pleased to oblige Bula Matari, and with his persuasions added, Magwala was induced to consent to the truce.

Irebu was situated on the south bank of the Congo, at the mouth of a creek called the Lukanga, in which little or no current was perceptible. Inquiry as to the cause elicited the information that there was "big water" higher up the creek; and it was further stated that from Irebu it was possible to reach Gankabi's village by ascending the Lukanga and crossing a lake called Mantumba, which at its farther extremity had water communication with Lake Leopold II. The news was interesting and exciting, but its verification had of necessity to be postponed to a more convenient season.

On June 8th the steamers reached the village of Inganda, situated near the mouth of a large tributary variously known as the Ikelemba, Baruki, and Molundu or Black River. This stream Stanley on his previous journey had supposed to be the principal tributary of the Congo : if so, a station at its mouth was manifestly desirable ; at any rate he proposed now to devote a day or two to exploring it.

The Black River, so called from the strong, tea-like colour of its water, proved much narrower than he had expected. Its banks were very low—so low, indeed, that in some places the water spread itself unchecked over considerable tracts of country. Then islands were seen; but it was evident that the river was in flood, as for some miles the banks were invisible, and all that could be seen were stretches of black water, backed by stretches of yet blacker forest. Villages seemed not to exist. On the second day the banks were higher, and here and there were settlements ; but though the inhabitants turned out in force to view the strangers, nowhere was any friendliness displayed. At one particularly pleasant-looking place an endeavour to open communication was made; but the attempt was nipped in the bud by one of the chiefs, who sternly announced his intention to fight should the strangers so much as approach the shore. In the face of such determined hostility, it was clearly useless to go on, so the *En Avant's* head was turned down-stream, the natives favouring the explorers with a parting salute of sticks and stones.

Making the best of his way back to the Congo, Stanley advanced as far as Wangata, seven miles above the junction of the Black River, and in the territory of the Bakuti tribe. These people gave the travellers a friendly welcome, and when blood brotherhood had been made with the customary ceremonies, land for building purposes was promised. But before a station could be commenced, it was necessary that the rest of the expedition, which had been left at Inganda, should be fetched up. A few men were therefore left at Wangata as pledges for the return of the others, and Stanley hurried off with the steamer to bring up the party from the camp.

At the site of the new station—to which, from its position, the name of Equator Station was given—the whole force remained several days, the men engaged in clearing the ground, and the officers in settling all necessary preliminaries. The command was then handed over to Lieutenant Vangele, to whom twenty-six men were assigned; while Lieutenant Coquilhat, with a smaller detachment, was detailed to assist him temporarily. Stanley then returned to Inganda, where a delicate task awaited him.

So favourable was the impression of the white men formed by the natives while the expedition was in camp at Inganda, that they were extremely anxious to have a station in their locality. But the place was too unhealthy from a European point of view for Stanley to venture on anything of the sort. Yet if he refused how was he to avoid giving dire offence, as his reason for doing so would certainly not be understood ? Mswenne, the Mswata man, undertook to find a way out of the difficulty ; and this he most ingeniously did by attiring himself in the garb of woe, and then, in broken tones, telling of a wholly imaginary attack on the expedition, in which a Zanzibari was killed, and a lad from Irebu captured. They must go at once, he insisted, to avenge the dead and captured men ; and at this point in his story the wily fellow became so overcome that he howled aloud. The tale, which bore every appearance of truth, was so well told that the desired station was forgotten, and the simple folk of Inganda offered their assistance in the threatened war of vengeance. Their offer, of course, was gratefully declined, and under cover of their sympathy the expedition got away and returned to Irebu.

While the boats were being made fast the sound

of firing was heard, and Stanley was informed that the chiefs, having tired of waiting, had resumed the war. He promptly visited Mangombo, who said he had no desire to fight; and then sent Dualla to learn Mpika's views on the subject. He also, it seemed, was willing to make peace; so Dualla was sent out, with the Association flag as a safe conduct, to make known to the hostile forces in the field that Bula Matari had come, and was ready to hold the peace palaver.

The conference took place on the following day, when each chief stated his grievances. No one apparently expected to gain any good by continuing the war, and Stanley pointed out that the only possible result of a continuance of the strife would be the weakening of all the Irebu villages to such an extent that some other tribe would be able to swoop down on them and seize their country. This was a view of the case which had not previously presented itself to the chiefs, but they saw its truth, and after some further discussion, agreed to abide by Bula Matari's decision, and to pay him a fee of a hundred and twenty brass rods for acting as judge. Stanley thereupon gave judgment that the war must cease, and forthwith all the villages sent in pledges of peace, in the shape of calico, palm wine, damp gunpowder, and broken guns. The latter, with much firing of muskets, were solemnly buried on the battle-ground, in token that the war was dead, and that peace had come to life.

CHAPTER VIII.

FARTHER AFIELD.

TWO days after the peace celebrations Stanley explored the Lukanga River. It was a sluggish stream, and, properly speaking, scarcely to be called a river, but was rather a channel connecting the shallow Mantumba Lake with the Congo. The channel itself varied in width from about three hundred yards in its narrowest part to a lakelike expansion, which again contracted to a winding, sedge-grown waterway, and this, in turn, opened out into the Mantumba Lake. This, though the deepest sounding obtained was only thirty-two feet, was a fairly large sheet of water, containing numerous picturesque bays and inlets, and occupying a hollow formed apparently by the subsidence of a tract of ironstone rock. The scenery on the shores presented great variety. Here were rugged edges of rock, presenting signs of fracture as clear and sharp as though the subsidence had just taken place ; there pebbly beaches ; and yet again, forest-clad hills and slopes rising gradually from the dark, inky-looking waters of the lake. No connection with Lake Leopold was apparent; but seeing that the southern shore was low and sedgy, it was quite conceivable that in the wet season, when rivers and lakes were in flood, it might be, as the natives had said, quite possible for canoes to travel from the one lake to the other.

Two days were devoted to the exploration of the lake, and then returning to the Congo, Stanley proceeded down-stream to Lukolela, where he halted for a few hours, to secure a plot of land for a station and make brotherhood with the two chiefs Iuka and Mungawa.

At Mswata, where the next halt was made, all was well. During Stanley's absence Abbé Guyot, a Roman Catholic missionary, had arrived on the scene, and it now transpired that, finding the ground at Leopoldville already occupied by two missions—one Baptist, the other undenominational—he had decided to go on to Mswata. Stanley suggested the mouth of the Kwa as a suitable field for his labours, and as the abbé professed himself pleased with the suggestion, he requested Lieutenant Janssen to form a new station on the near bank of the Kwa, and help the abbé to establish his mission on the farther bank.

After four days' halt steam was got up, and the journey towards Leopoldville was continued. A call at Kimpoko, near the head of Stanley Pool, was less satisfactory than the visit to Mswata had been.

Nothing was completed, and in the few months that had elapsed since the station was founded four officers had had charge. The place seemed doomed to ill-luck, especially when contrasted with Leopoldville, where now all was going well. Had this not been so the outlook would have seemed black indeed. Kimpoko could hardly be considered anything but a failure; and now bad news arrived from Bwabwa Njali's village, where a new station was in course of construction. A young officer full of hope and courage had been put in charge; but the poor fellow had not been many days at work when he went out of his mind, and believing that his men had conspired to murder him, fired at Bwabwa Njali, and also at his own sergeant, whom he wounded in the head. On this the men disarmed and bound him; but during the night he managed to free himself and escape to the forest, where next day he was recaptured. News of the disturbance reached Leopoldville, and a party sent to make inquiries arrived just in time to convey the unfortunate madman back to the principal station, whence he was sent down to Vivi.

Scarcely was this affair settled when from Mswata came the sad news that Lieutenant Janssen and Abbé Guyot had both been drowned. The natives had warned them that a storm was brewing; but confident, probably, in their own powers of navigation, they persisted in making the attempt to travel by boat from Kwamouth to Mswata. As predicted, the storm came on long before they reached their destination; the boat upset, and both perished in the raging stream.

Kimpoko next fell into trouble, for the officer in charge came into collision with the natives, several of whom were shot. Stanley, of course, hurried up to see what was wrong, and found on his arrival that the natives, scared by their defeat, had fled from the neighbourhood. He could not induce them to return, and as a station in an uninhabited region would be useless, he destroyed the building, and took the garrison back to Leopoldville. Thus within a few days two unfinished stations came to grief—a bitter disappointment.

About three weeks later came the news that Bolobo station had been completely destroyed by fire, and Stanley once more started up-stream, taking with him a miscellaneous cargo of goods. On arriving at Bolobo he found things in even worse plight than he had been led to expect. There, staring him in the face, were the blackened ruins; and while he was listening to an account of the fire, a messenger from Ibaka, the senior chief, informed him that two of the minor chiefs had opened fire on the steamers, although, as the boats came up, every kind of friendly demonstration had been made. Steam was hastily got up, and the *En Avant*, with Stanley and Mr. Glave, a young Englishman who was to take

charge of the new station at Lukolela, hurried off
to the scene of conflict. In a few moments the
En Avant also was under fire, and rifles were fetched
up and a few volleys discharged into the bushes
whence the native fire proceeded. As quickly as
might be, the boats were convoyed to the landing-
place, the goods were unloaded, and then the *Royal*
was sent off to Leopoldville to fetch up a Krupp
gun, with an artillery officer to take charge of it.

Meanwhile the war continued—harmlessly so far
as results to the expedition were concerned, and
without serious injury to the hostile natives, only
two of whom were killed, though several others were
injured. The fact that a chief was among the
wounded seemed, however, to depress them. They
came to ask for peace, and offered a war indemnity,
which, however, was so trifling that they were told
they must pay more heavily for the luxury of shooting at unoffending people. Unless they chose to pay
an adequate fine, the rifle fire would continue until
the big gun should come up and blow them and
their village up to the sky. At this terrible prospect the minor chiefs immediately put themselves
into Ibaka's hands ; but even then it took him nine
days to induce them to pay the fine demanded—
namely, six hundred brass rods, valued at £15.

On the day following the proclamation of peace
the Krupp arrived, and at once became the centre
of attraction, though no one would believe it was

really a gun, inasmuch as it lacked the stock, ram-
rod, and trigger, with which all the old-fashioned
muskets known at Bolobo were provided. By way
of enlightening the unbelievers, the gun was loaded,
sighted to two thousand yards, and discharged into
the Congo, raising such a column of water that the
death-dealing power of the Krupp remained no longer
a matter for doubt. A second shot at three thousand
yards' range produced a similar effect; and then the
power of the gun being fully vindicated, Stanley
celebrated the occasion by presenting each of the
chiefs and headmen with a piece of cloth and ten
brass rods. The gift produced a palaver, followed
by a demand for more cloth and rods; but these
Stanley declined to give, and turning to Dualla,
ordered him to gather up the original presents. He
had had enough, he said, and would leave Bolobo
for ever. This decided reply at once brought the
chiefs to their bearings. They explained that their
demand had only been made in accord with native
custom: would not Bula Matari put away his
anger? The trouble was ended: they loved money,
and had already lost too much by fighting; hence-
forward they wished to live at peace with the white
men.

Tranquillity was thus restored, and there being
no further need for delay, on September 16th the
pioneers re-embarked, and six days later arrived at
Lukolela, Glave's future station. At that stage it

could not be said to look very promising, for the land assigned to the expedition was densely wooded with tall trees, beneath which the ground was covered with brush and small bushes. The timber was particularly fine. Many of the trees were a hundred and fifty feet in height, and among the varieties in the immediate neighbourhood of the station were teak, plane, mahogany, redwood, and guaiacum, all of first-rate quality, and fit for every sort of work, from cabinetmaking to shipbuilding. Yet, to Stanley's surprise, the ground was by no means as rich as the quality of the timber led him to expect. The bulk of it was hard ironstone conglomerate, on which picks made little or no impression.

As soon as Glave and his men had made a good start at Lukolela, the bulk of the expedition started off again up-stream to Equator Station, where, during Stanley's absence of just over three months, the two lieutenants in charge had indeed worked wonders. They had constructed a commodious house, well supplied with furniture—also their own handiwork— and had even gone in for decorative effects ingeniously produced with the aid of a few yards of baize, print, and sheeting of various colours. The men, inspired by the example of their officers, had followed suit to the best of their ability in the erection of their own houses, while the gardens also presented a most thriving appearance.

Even at that pleasant spot no long stay could be

made, and in a few days the expedition was once more afloat, on its way to its ultimate destination at Stanley Falls, some six hundred miles ahead. Here and there, at likely-looking villages, a call was made, and if the negotiations were satisfactory Stanley seldom left the place without having entered into brotherhood with its chief. Thus, after some days' steaming, he came to Iboko, the territory of the warlike Bangala tribe, who had given him an unpleasantly warm reception when he passed down the Congo in 1877. What now to expect at their hands he knew not; for while some of the natives averred that they were ready to dispute every inch of the way, others stated that they had no wish again to try conclusions with Stanley.

As the steamers passed their villages they gathered quietly on the banks, and though no warlike preparations were visible, neither was any sign of friendliness to be seen. At last three canoes shot out, and as the *En Avant* steamed forward alone to meet them, the Bangala shouted an inquiry as to what the strangers wanted. Yumbila, a Usindi man, who had accompanied the expedition as guide and interpreter, bawled in return the news that Bula Matari had come to see the chief, Mata Bwyki (the Master of Many Guns). He, it seemed, was not at home, but Boliko, another chief, was in his village. Having vouchsafed this scanty information, the canoemen darted back, and the steamers puffed steadily onward along the front of this immense settlement, where for many miles village succeeded village in rapid succession.

The tidings that Bula Matari had come in peace were rapidly noised abroad, and in a wonderfully short time canoes of every size and description crowded round the steamers. Evidently the Bangala had decided not to fight, but as a matter of prudence Stanley decided not to land at any of the villages, but to take up his quarters for the night on a dreary islet opposite Boliko's village. Thence Yumbila departed in a canoe to visit Boliko, whom, about sunset, he brought back with him to the camp. The chief was a well-built young fellow, with a somewhat furtive expression, but in manner he was cordial enough, and offered to introduce Stanley to Mata Bwyki. Then he went back to his village, and the pioneers got through the night as best they could in a damp and comfortless camp.

In the morning Boliko came with forty canoes to escort them to his village, where a lively trade began. Provisions were very cheap, and a good store had been laid in by the time that messengers from Mata Bwyki brought word that the senior chief felt himself somewhat aggrieved that such important visitors should be the guests of a young chief like Boliko. Another chief named Ndingda, however, managed to soothe the ruffled feelings of the senior, and he

H.L.Bacon.

Parleying with the Aruwimi Natives.

ended by inviting the strangers to call on him the next day.

During the night another trait of Bangala character was manifested. Honesty was evidently not their strong point, and under cover of the darkness expert thieves visited the camp. Again and again were the sleepers disturbed by shouts from one or another who awakened to find his property gone, and the return of daylight revealed many thefts which during the darkness had been undetected. It was the first time anything of the sort had occurred, and the men were not a little disgusted at their manifold losses. But as crying over spilt milk is always useless, the thefts were allowed to pass unnoticed, and the defrauded travellers steamed a couple of miles down-stream to Mata Bwyki's village, where they were greeted by an overpowering stench of decomposing cassava from the stagnant pits in which the bitter roots were steeped with the view of extracting the poisonous juice. Near this savoury spot the travellers made their first acquaintance with Mata Bwyki. He was a fine-looking man of commanding stature, and though apparently well on for eighty years of age, owned a clear, strong voice, which could be heard without difficulty at several hundred yards' distance. With him were his sons and grandsons, all tall, well-built fellows, and around them were grouped the villagers, old and young, who, in their anxiety for a near view of

the wonderful white men, gathered so closely round
the mats spread for the palaver that it became
difficult to breathe.

As Stanley understood not a word of the language
of Iboko, the duty of speech-making rested on
Yumbila, who stated at some length the objects of
the expedition, and then gave the chiefs a sketch
of the work already accomplished. Towns had been
built, he said, at many places, and all along the
course of the river the principal chiefs had made
blood brotherhood with Bula Matari, who was otherwise known as "Tandelay." Would not Mata Bwyki
do likewise ?

That Bula Matari was one and the same with
"Tandelay," who had signally beaten the Bangala
in 1877, was news to Mata Bwyki, and for a few
moments the decision whether there should be war
or peace seemed to hang in the balance. But Yumbila took up his parable once more, and went on to
tell how Bula Matari had made peace at Irebu, of
his wonderful guns with their lengthy range and
mighty voices, of the rich goods which he possessed,
and the many other marvels which had taken place
since the white man came up the river. Mata Bwyki
listened to all in silence, and when Yumbila ceased
speaking a forked palm branch was brought. Kokoro,
Mata Bwyki's eldest son, came forward, took hold
of one twig himself, asked Stanley to grasp the other,
and then lifting his short sword, split the branch in

two. This, according to Bangala custom, was the sign that he wished to make blood brotherhood, and in a few moments another member was added to Stanley's rapidly growing family of brothers. At the conclusion of the usual ceremony Mata Bwyki made a speech, and called on the assembled people to regard Bula Matari as a brother and a member of the tribe from that day forward, inasmuch as he and their chief had made blood brotherhood. Bula Matari's people were thenceforth to be their people; the Bangala were not to steal from them nor hurt them; they were to trade fairly and honestly, and to live in peace one with the other. Following up this friendly beginning, Stanley promised to return after a time and found a station, of which he intended to give Lieutenant Coquilhat the charge; though first, as he explained, he must go on farther to reconnoitre. Presents were then exchanged, and after two days' stay the visit was brought to a close, and the expedition once more went aboard, to continue the voyage through a perfect archipelago of islands clad with the most gorgeous tropical vegetation.

Several days were passed in winding in and out among all this wealth of beauty, and then, towards the close of a glorious day, the sky became overcast with unusual blackness. Darker and darker it grew as cloud rolled up after cloud, and soon no doubt remained that a terrific storm was brewing. Every one looked out for shelter; but in the dense bush which clothed the bank no opening could be seen, and the boats perforce kept on their way along a river whose surface was absolutely still, while no breath of air stirred the tiniest leaf.

Then with startling suddenness came the wind— a wild, whirling blast, awaking the thousand voices of the forest, dashing the calm surface of the river into countless waves, and forcibly driving the steamers down-stream. In another moment down rushed the rain in sheets and torrents, half drowning the luckless pioneers, as with their boat-hooks they grappled the bushes, to save themselves from being driven back by the force of the storm. As darkness closed in, however, the rain ceased, and one of the men found an opening in the bush where it was possible to climb ashore, camp, and make fast the hawsers.

During the next few days the course lay through magnificent forests of gum-copal trees, from whose tops depended wreaths of orchella weed, valuable for the rich dye which it produces. Two or three deserted villages were passed, and daily the islands which studded the river seemed to become more numerous and complicated, while the rising waters in many places added to the difficulties of navigation by overflowing their banks, and wandering off into the forest. Still no sign of human life was seen until, on November 1st, the expedition reached Nganza, with whose chief, Rubunga, Stanley had made acquaintance when he came down the Congo six years before. Here the people were anxious to trade, and seemed terribly disappointed when they found that by no blandishments could the pioneers be induced to buy ivory. This country was known to the down-stream natives as Langa-Langa, and the absolute nudity fashionable in the locality came as rather a shock to the pioneers. A somewhat elaborate tattoo pattern was the nearest approach made by either man or woman to clothing ; cloth was, therefore, valueless, and black and white beads resembling fragments of pipe stems were the only form of currency in demand. But as fashions change, the sight of clothing worn by others probably produced the desire to imitate, and before the pioneers left the village a brisk demand for bright handkerchiefs, and even for pieces of rag, sprang up.

On November 7th a halt was made at Bumba, a large townlike settlement, where for the fiftieth time Stanley made brotherhood. The people were evidently disposed to be friendly, but at the same time they were greatly in dread of an evil spirit known as the Ibanza, who was popularly supposed to be concealed in the " smoke-boats," where he puffed, panted, and sobbed, as all could see and hear. Suppose the Ibanza were to escape from his confinement, what would he do ? Was it safe to trade with the people connected with him ? Evidently the point was doubtful, for although provisions were abundant, the people were at first too frightened to approach.

Fortunately, the prevailing alarm did not extend to the chiefs. On the second day, therefore, some trade was done; but at the least sound from the engine, or unexpected movement of the white men, a general panic ensued, and off went the natives in headlong haste. Then, when all seemed safe, back they would come, wearing, however, restless, uneasy expressions, indicative of their readiness to fly at the slightest provocation.

Taking advantage of their nervousness, a mischievous cabin-boy dressed himself up in a tiger skin which formed part of the cabin furniture of the *En Avant.* Presently the door was thrown open, and out crept the tiger in full view of the multitude. Some one caught sight of the apparition, and raised a yell, and the whole crowd, after one hasty look, fled, yelling and shrieking, from the Ibanza, who at last had manifested himself. For a moment the pioneers were puzzled: what on earth was the matter now? But when the object of terror was discovered a roar of laughter arose. The jovial sounds reached the flying natives, and speedily brought them to a halt. Evidently thinking that the Ibanza could not, after all, be so very terrible, back they came; and then, as they learned the real nature of the bogy, they too burst into shouts of laughter.

A few miles above Bumba was another populous village called Yambinga, a little to the north of which a large tributary called, variously, the Itimbiri and the Ngingiri joined the Congo. Here several hundreds of war canoes were seen; and as Bumba possessed about four hundred, and one or two other villages in the neighbourhood owned an equal number, the united fleets totalled up to well over a thousand vessels—a formidable array to tackle. But now all was well, and without let or hindrance the expedition steamed past the delta of the Itimbiri to Mutembo, a group of palisaded villages, whose inhabitants, expecting evidently to be attacked, greeted the steamers with a futile demonstration of hostility.

Five days later (November 15th), at the mouth of the Aruwimi, a number of war canoes came out, and while the drums thundered the call to arms hundreds of fully armed warriors of the Basoko tribe lined the banks. In order not to provoke attack, the smaller steamers were moored at a clearing on the opposite side of the Aruwimi, while the *En Avant*, with Yumbila on board, hurried across the stream to convey assurances of peace and good will to the assembled warriors. What the guide said was unintelligible to the white men; but to the people of Mokulu it was convincing, for the war shouts ceased, the drums became silent, and a sudden and complete stillness succeeded the warlike din. Weapons were laid aside, and then, as Yumbila continued to speak words of peace and friendship, a kindly answer came. Would the strangers, inquired the speaker, be pleased to return to their camp on the farther shore? If so, he and his people would come there in peace to make acquaintance.

With this reasonable request Stanley, of course, complied, and a small party of Basoko paddled shyly up. For a long time they could not be induced to land, but at length they summoned up courage to come ashore and make brotherhood with sundry members of the expedition. Shouts and yells of joy carried the good news to Mokulu, and the drums once more lifted up their voices, but this time their message was of friendship and peace.

That evening Yumbila crossed to Mokulu and spent the night with the villagers, who told him a strange tale of a tribe led by a pale-faced man, who some years before had come down the Congo. The Basoko, concluding that the errand of the strangers was not one of peace, sallied out in their war canoes; but as they bore down on the strangers a shower of fire and "soft iron" cut them to pieces, though no man could see how his brethren were slain. Then the strangers went away, and the dreadful booming which had accompanied the death-dealing shower was heard no more in the land until a few days before Stanley's arrival.

Then, early one morning, before it was light, the

dreaded sound awakened the sleepers in the village,
and rushing out they found many of the huts in
flames, a whizzing and buzzing was heard, and many
of the people were struck dead in the same mysterious way as those who were slain by the strange
tribe with the white-faced leader. Terrified almost
to death the survivors ran for their lives to the
woods, whence they looked out at the destruction,
and thought of showing fight. But hearing the
shrieks of captured women and children, and the
booming of the death tubes, and seeing the still
burning houses, even the warriors dared not come
out, and they lay still until silence fell over the
scene of battle. Then venturing forth, they found
half the village in ruins, while hundreds of the women
and children who had failed to escape had vanished.

By the tribe led by the pale-faced man Stanley's
expedition which came down the Congo in 1877 was
probably meant, but who could these recent raiders
be ? Slave-dealers no doubt : if so, whence came
they ? No one saw them come, and no one saw
them go ; the only thing tolerably certain was that
they had not come up the Congo. Nor could any
information be obtained respecting the Aruwimi ;
even its local name, Biyerré, was not revealed ; and
the disclosure of Stanley's intention to explore it
nearly caused a breach of the peace, though no
objection was made to his going up the Congo. He
declined, however, to be turned from his purpose,

and the next three days were spent in ascending the tributary. Ninety-six miles of the stream were explored, and then, as a series of rapids blocked the way, the steamers halted at Yambuya, a village just below the rapids.

Here Yumbila endeavoured to induce the people to trade; but though they were willing to talk for any length of time, they stoutly declared they had not anything to sell—in fact, they were starving. This, though manifestly untrue, was all that could be got out of them ;- **no** blandishments had any effect, and finally the attempt to trade was given up in disgust. It was clear that no reliance could be placed on anything they might say, for their statements did not tally with those of their neighbours, who called the river Biyerré, while, according to these people, it was the Massua, Kiyo, or Ikongo. Time, however, would not allow of further investigation, though what the upper course of the stream might be was an interesting problem. Stanley was disposed to think it might be identical with the Welle, which had been partially explored by Dr. Schweinfurth; but this was mere speculation. For the present, at least, his duty lay on the Congo, and on November 23rd he was back at Mokulu, preparatory to continuing his journey up the great river.

CHAPTER IX.

AMONG THE SLAVE-RAIDERS.

AS the expedition passed on, the evidences of recent fighting—or, more probably, of the depredations of slave-dealers—became more and more apparent. On November 24th several market-places were seen, but all were silent and deserted, while the few natives visible hurried away to some hiding-place as soon as the steamers appeared. A little later a long line of canoes, possibly a thousand in all, was seen slinking cautiously along under cover of the thick overhanging bushes on an island. Did they intend to fight? If so, their numbers were overwhelming; but there soon proved to be no need for apprehension, for the canoemen seemed only anxious to escape notice.

Then came more deserted villages. Some of these had been recently destroyed by fire, and the scorched trees and ragged, miserable-looking banana groves gave evidence of the fierceness of the flames. Here and there, too, for some inscrutable reason, a few long canoes had been reared up on end. This could scarcely be the work of natives, and Stanley argued, therefore, that a gang of Arab slave-raiders was somewhere in the neighbourhood, and that this apparently senseless freak was an evidence of their presence. The impression was soon confirmed, for a few miles farther up a group of disheartened, dejected natives were seen crouching miserably on the bank, too wretched to care even to run away.

With these people Yumbila managed to communicate, and finding he was a friend, they opened their hearts, and told how, a few days before, their village had been raided, their houses burned, their friends slain or carried off, and almost all they possessed destroyed. The survivors were living as best they could, hiding during the day amongst the islands, with their canoes ready for instant flight, and at night stealing cautiously to their fields to get food. It was a pitiful tale; but what could the pioneers do? Living, as they were, from hand to mouth, they could only speak a few kind words, and pass on through further scenes of woe towards their goal.

On November 27th, what from the distance had looked like a smudge of white on the river banks, resolved itself into the tents of the slavers' camp. Why not fall upon the miscreants and avenge the wrongs of the hapless villagers whom they had slain, enslaved, or ruined? But—so Stanley argued with himself—what right had he to constitute himself their champion and avenger? Further, his errand was peace, not war; and deciding to remain neutral, he visited the slavers' camp, where over two thousand wretched beings were chained, to await the time when they could be conveyed to Nyangwe and other Arab settlements above Stanley Falls. The ground was littered with plunder of every description, and the whole scene was one of misery too great for words to describe.

Stanley Falls were now not far distant, and on December 2, 1883, five days after leaving the slave camp, the lowest of the seven cataracts which make up the Falls was sighted. Early in the afternoon of that day the steamers were moored near a fishing village on a small island just below the cataract, and a palaver was held with the view of obtaining land to found a station. At first, judging by the hubbub which ensued when the interpreters had finished speaking, the idea did not find favour, and for a while the utmost confusion prevailed. Then the meeting subsided into quietness, and one after another spoke, apparently discussing the pros and cons of the affair. Those who agreed with the remarks of any speaker expressed their approval by arranging his grass-cloth garments, while the dissentients howled and raved in derision. Public feeling was clearly unsettled, and to arrive at any conclusion seemed difficult—in fact, before a decision was reached the meeting tired itself out, and adjourned until the following day.

When the palaver reassembled, the question of selling land was still undecided—some were for, others against the transaction—and the discussion waxed fast and furious, until those in favour of the sale finally prevailed. A price was fixed, and at the conclusion of the palaver Stanley handed over goods to the value of about £160, whereupon the islands and a strip of land on the left bank of the Congo were formally ceded to him. All that remained to be done was to build the station, and as a convenient site on one of the islands had been selected while the palaver was in progress, all hands immediately set to work to clear the ground.

Scarcely was the work begun when the gentleman who had come up for the express purpose of taking charge of the station found that the post was by no means to his liking, and he begged to be released from his agreement. Fortunately, a substitute was speedily forthcoming; for Mr. Binnie, a Scotsman, who hitherto had been serving as engineer of the *Royal*, expressed a wish to fill the vacancy. He was a little fellow, slight and delicate in appearance, but his pluck was undeniable; and the fact that after all the hardships of the journey he still desired to remain in the wilds went far to prove his fitness for the post. He therefore received the desired appointment, and thirty-one men were left with him to build and garrison the new station.

The other members of the expedition, having done

their work, bade their comrades farewell, and on
December 10th set out on the homeward journey.
Running down-stream with the current was a very
different matter from struggling up against it, and
the distance to the slavers' camp, which, on the
upward journey, had taken over three days, was
now covered in little more than the same number
of hours. A halt was again made, and Stanley,
remembering that one of the ulterior objects of
the Association was the suppression of the slave-
trade, invited the raiders to send a few of their
confidential men on a trip to the coast. His idea
was that if they saw the work in progress on the
Congo it might occur to them that it was unwise
to pursue their operations in a locality where at any
time they might meet a patrolling gunboat. This,
however, he did not express in so many words, and
considering it wiser to leave them to make their
own inferences, contented himself with pointing out
that the opportunity of doing a little trade was a
favourable one, as they could send some ivory to
the coast, and purchase with the proceeds any
articles they might chance to require.

The invitation was accepted, and on December 12th
the steamers, with their cargo increased by thirty
tusks of ivory, once more got under way. Ten
Arabs were also added to the passenger list, and
from them Stanley obtained a good deal of information respecting the country through which they were

passing, and the various tributaries which emptied themselves into the Congo.

Sundry villages were visited, and at each of them one or more of the principal men joined Stanley's rapidly-increasing assortment of " brothers ; " but no long halts were made until December 15th, when an accident to the *Royal* caused four days' delay. The steamers were crossing from the left to the right bank, when the *Royal* struck a submerged snag, and began to settle down. With all speed her cargo and passengers were transferred to the other boats, and it was then discovered that, as she was fast caught on the snag, she was in no immediate danger. Accordingly further operations were deferred until the following morning, when, after some trouble, she was released.

By the morning of December 20th the expedition was once more afloat, and later in the day a halt was made at Upoto, with the object of obtaining provisions, making brotherhood with the chiefs, and, as the place promised well for a future station, purchasing some land. Treaties were also concluded with several neighbouring chiefs, and a good deal of useful work was done before Equator Station was reached (December 29th). Here all was prosperous, and a flourishing avenue of bananas, along with several other improvements, testified to the untiring energy of the two officers in charge.

New Year's Day 1884 found Stanley, accom-

A Slave Raid.

panied by Lieutenant Coquilhat, once more ascending the Congo to revisit Iboko. This trip was, however, a mere temporary break in his westward journey; for on January 10th he was once more on his way down-stream, visiting station after station as he passed westward. Lukolela was doing well, and its chief, Mr. Glave, looked the picture of health and strength, though, owing to the natural difficulties of the site, he had done a good deal of hard work, and had plenty more before him. Bolobo, however, was less prosperous. It had again been completely destroyed by fire, the conflagration on this occasion being the work of a delirious and dying man, who, as it appeared, desired that his obsequies should be celebrated by a grand blaze. It was impossible to arrest the flames, for not only were the walls and thatch dry as tinder, but the explosion of the shells and cartridges stored in the magazine rendered it dangerous to approach. The men, therefore, were forced to watch the destruction without being able to lift a finger to save their property. There was nothing for it but to rebuild the station, and Lieutenant Liebrechts, the officer in charge, a man not easily discouraged, set about the work with undaunted energy.

At Kwamouth and Kinshassa all was well, while Leopoldville, under Lieutenant Valcke, was as prosperous and peaceful as Stanley could desire; even Ngalyema now acted in a reasonable and consist-

ently friendly manner. No special events marked
the remainder of the journey, and early in April
Stanley arrived at Vivi, where, as usual, nothing
was satisfactory. No progress had been made—in
fact, things were worse rather than better; and
seeing no hope of improvement, Stanley decided to
remove the station bodily to the larger plateau.
The work was begun immediately, although Stanley's
stay on the Congo was rapidly approaching its conclusion. He had indeed expected to find his successor awaiting him at Vivi; but General Gordon,
who had accepted the post, withdrew at the last
moment, as his own Government needed his services
at Khartum, and it was not until early in May that
his substitute, Colonel de Winton, arrived on the
scene. During the month Stanley spent at Vivi after
the colonel's arrival the new station made rapid
progress, and everything looked hopeful, when, on
June 6th, the pioneer of the Congo Free State, having
handed over his work to others, embarked on the
first stage of his voyage to Europe.

CHAPTER X.

TO HELP EMIN.

IN 1876, while Stanley was commencing his first exploration of the Congo, and General (then Colonel) Gordon was serving under the Egyptian Government in the Sudan, Dr. Edward Schnitzer, a German Jew, better known by his assumed name of Emin, also entered the Egyptian service. He was sent down to join Gordon, who quickly recognized his merits, and, two years later, appointed him governor of the Equatorial Province. Here he laboured more or less successfully, until in 1883 the extending power of the Mahdi cut him off from all communication with the outside world. From that time he was left entirely to himself. Gordon was shut up in Khartum, and was unable to render him any assistance, and the Egyptian Government appeared to have forgotten his existence. No shadow of attempt was made to reach him, and in 1885, finding that his position was untenable, he retreated southward, and established himself at Wadelai, a little to the north of the Albert Nyanza.

From this place the unfortunate governor, abandoned by the Government in whose service he was supposed to be engaged, and disregarded by his German countrymen, wrote to various private individuals stating his case, and asking them, if possible, to obtain assistance for him. Some of these letters were published in the *Times*, but no Government seemed disposed to take up the matter. Finally, several private individuals formed a Committee, and raised a relief fund, with the view of sending an expedition to rescue Emin. Stanley was consulted on the matter, and expressed his willingness to lead the proposed expedition, if the Committee desired that he should do so; or, if they did not require his services, to contribute £500 to the funds.

Four routes were proposed, but three of them—from the east coast—were, in Stanley's opinion, undesirable. In the first place, by any of them it would be necessary to pass through more or less hostile country; secondly, the risk of desertions from the ranks of the porters was very great, as from almost any point on these routes they would have little difficulty in returning to their own country as soon as they became tired of the hardships of the journey; thirdly, the Masailand route suggested by Mr. Joseph Thompson, who had explored that country, presented special difficulties on account of the scarcity both of food and water. Stanley proposed that the longer but much easier route by the Congo should be adopted, inasmuch as both food and water were plentiful, and water transit could be obtained for the greater part of the distance. His idea was to purchase a number of whaleboats, which could be conveyed in sections from the coast to Stanley Pool; and this he believed would be practically the chief difficulty of the Congo route. Of course, it would be necessary to obtain the consent of King Leopold to the passage of the expedition through the Congo Free State, but in doing this no difficulty was anticipated.

Having laid the pros and cons of the various routes before the Committee, Stanley departed to America, where he had arranged to deliver a series of lectures on his work on the Congo. He had only been there a fortnight, when he received a message from Sir William Mackinnon, informing him that his plan and offer were accepted, and asking him to return at once to England, as the matter was urgent. This, of course, compelled him to cancel his engagements in America, and returning by the first available steamer, he landed in England on Christmas Eve 1884. He then found that, though Mackinnon had cabled that his plan was accepted, the members of the Committee preferred one of the eastern routes. Stanley replied that the decision rested with them, and he proceeded to make arrangements to obtain porters, provisions, trade goods, and donkeys at Zanzibar. These were to be sent forward to the mission station at Mpwapwa, about two hundred miles to the westward of Zanzibar, where he proposed to join them.

Meanwhile he was busily engaged in England in laying in stores, provisions, arms, and ammunition, and in selecting the European members of the expedition from a crowd of eager applicants. Finally, he chose Lieutenant Stairs, a young officer of Engineers, who obtained special leave of absence from his regiment; Mr. Bonny, a well-drilled soldier, recently of the Army Medical Department; Mr. Troup, who had been for some time in the service of the Congo Free State; Major Barttelot, an eager, hardworking officer of the 7th Fusiliers; Captain Nelson, who had seen hard service in Zululand; Mr. Jameson, who, besides having already had considerable experience of African travel, was a large contributor to the relief fund; and Mr. Jephson, who, as yet, had had no experience of travel, rough work, or hardship.

Early in January, Sir William Mackinnon had a letter from King Leopold, expressing his strong desire that the expedition should travel by way of the Congo. All arrangements had been made with the view of taking the east coast route, but on receipt of his Majesty's letter the matter was reconsidered, and Stanley was again consulted. He pointed out some half-dozen reasons which made the Congo route preferable to any other; and finally, as the British Government undertook to transport the expedition from Zanzibar to the Congo mouth, and King Leopold offered the use of his boats on the river, it was decided that the change should be made, though it was now too late to order the whaleboats. This alteration of plans involved a good deal of extra work and expense; but by the end of the third week in January everything was in train, and the 27th of that month found Stanley at Cairo. Here he engaged a new member of the expedition, in the person of Surgeon Parke, of the British Army Medical Department, and also obtained official letters authorizing Emin Pasha and the troops under his command either to retire with the relief expedition, or to remain in the Sudan, as they might prefer. Only, in the event of any one electing to remain, it was clearly stated that the Government would neither accept the responsibility nor send any further relief.

Sixty-one Sudanese soldiers were detailed for service with the expedition, and with these and his European staff Stanley sailed from Aden on February 12th. Ten days later he was at Zanzibar, where he found that his agents had worked so energetically that very little remained to be done. There were, however, a few people to be interviewed, and among them Tippu Tib, an adventurous Arab, who, having amassed a fortune by slave-dealing, had rendered Stanley material assistance in his exploration of the Congo in 1877, and had since extended his power, until he had become practically king of the whole

region between Tanganyika Lake and Stanley Falls.
It was therefore most desirable to secure his good
will; so, as Emin was credited with the possession
of about £60,000 worth of ivory, Stanley arranged
with Tippu Tib to supply porters to assist in conveying the ammunition and other stores to Emin,
and then to bring back the ivory to the Falls.   This
business disposed of, Stanley made a further proposition—namely, that Tippu Tib should take charge
at Stanley Falls, where, after the departure of Mr.
Binnie and his immediate successor, everything had
gone wrong. A quarrel with the Arabs had led to
the destruction of the station; and as a result, the
districts below the Falls were at the mercy of the
slavers, who were fast devastating the neighbourhood. On the principle, therefore, of setting a thief
to catch a thief, Stanley, being authorized by King
Leopold to do so, offered Tippu Tib a regular salary
to act as governor of the Falls Station, on the understanding that he was neither to indulge in slave-
raiding himself, nor allow any one else to do so.
To this scheme Tippu Tib joyfully assented, and on
February 25th, when the expedition sailed from
Zanzibar, he and his followers were included in the
party.

The voyage occupied about three weeks, and on
March 18th the expedition landed at Banana Point,
where Stanley at once set about finding means of
transport to Matadi, on the south side of the Congo,

nearly opposite Vivi. He was fortunate enough to obtain three steamers, and to these men, goods, and animals were transferred immediately. On the 21st Matadi was reached, and the next few days were spent in unloading the goods and preparing to march overland to Leopoldville. If rumours prevalent at Banana Point were correct, the steamers at Stanley Pool were in very bad condition. The *Stanley* was said to be a perfect ruin, the *Royal* rotten, while the *En Avant* had been reduced to the status of a mere barge. This did not sound encouraging, and one of Stanley's first cares on reaching Matadi was to dispatch messengers to Leopoldville to request Lieutenant Liebrechts, who was now in charge at the Pool, to have the steamers repaired with all possible speed.

Early on the morning of March 25th the camp at Matadi was broken up, the Sudanese troops shouldered their rifles, the Zanzibari porters their loads, and shortly after six o'clock the expedition began its march. At first all went merrily, but the men, being completely out of training after their voyage, soon began to straggle. The furnace-like heat of the weather and the roughness and steepness of the road did not mend matters, and long before camping time Sudanese and Zanzibaris alike had lost all semblance of order, and were straggling along, grumbling as they went at the hardships they were called upon to endure. So much done up were

they that on the next day they were unable to go
forward, and a halt was made at Palaballa, one of
the stations of the Livingstone Inland Mission, where
the sick and weary were kindly tended by the missionaries. By the 28th they were again fit for work,
and the march was resumed. That day things went
on better, and a new recruit was engaged in the
person of Mr. Ward, who had been for some years
in the service of the Congo Free State, and seemed
likely to prove a useful addition to the staff.

During the next few days the heat and hard work
tried the men very much ; but the expedition wound
its weary way along the south bank of the Congo,
until, on April 22nd, much to the delight of all,
Leopoldville was safely reached. Here the men,
having finished their labours for the time being, had
nothing to do but rest ; but Stanley and other members of the staff found themselves with more than
enough to do in obtaining means of transport to
Yambuya, more than eleven hundred miles distant
on the Aruwimi, whence it would be necessary to
march overland to the Albert Nyanza. For the
whole distance to Yambuya the streams were navigable, but in the dilapidated condition of the steamers
on which Stanley had been reckoning for means of
transport what was to be done ? It was clear that
boats of some sort must be obtained, and in this
dilemma Mr. Billington of the Baptist Mission was
approached with the view of obtaining the loan of

the steamer *Henry Reed*. Mr. Bentley, of the same mission, had already, after a good deal of demur, consented to lend another of their steamers named the *Peace*.

At first Mr. Billington's reply was a decided refusal, and Barttelot and Jephson, who undertook to induce him to reconsider his decision, spent many hours in fruitless endeavours. Lieutenant Liebrechts then took the matter in hand; but he too was at first unsuccessful, and it was not until he had spent a whole day in going backwards and forwards with negotiations that Mr. Billington finally consented to hire out his steamer for the somewhat exorbitant charge of £100 per month.

In the meantime the *Stanley* had been put into working order, and now Mr. Swinburne, formerly Stanley's secretary and the governor of Vivi, offered the loan of the *Florida*, an incomplete steamer belonging to an ivory-trading company, of whose station at Kinshassa Swinburne was now manager. The *Florida* was minus engines and machinery, but the hull was completed, and if towed by one of the other steamers would serve as a barge. Stanley, gladly accepting the offer, marched the expedition down to Kinshassa to assist in launching the boat, and by April 30th everything was ready for the advance.

On May 1st the men were distributed among the boats, and the fleet steamed off; but scarcely was

the *Peace* well on her way when her rudder broke.
The current at that point was racing along at the
rate of six knots an hour, and as the boat began to
drift the captain dropped anchor—with disastrous
results, for the flimsy craft was unable to stand
the strain, and the anchor chains tore her deck to
pieces.   An attempt was made to haul up the anchors,
but they had fouled among the rocks, and all that
could be done was to cut the cable and drift back to
Kinshassa.   The engineers then set to work to repair
the damage; and this done, the *Peace* made another
start, and succeeded in reaching Kimpoko Station
at the head of Stanley Pool, where the rest of the
expedition was awaiting her arrival.

The order of advance was much the same as in
Stanley's previous voyage with the *En Avant* in
the service of the Free State.   Every evening about
five o'clock the boats were moored, a camp was
formed, and the men turned out in parties to fetch
in wood to be chopped up by firelight for the morrow's
steaming.   This work sometimes occupied several
hours; but until it was completed, and the wood
duly stacked on board, the day's work was not at
an end.   Then came a few hours' sleep, but early
in the morning every one was astir in order to get
off in good time.

Progress, however, was provokingly slow, owing
chiefly to the vagaries of the *Peace*.   Every forty-
five minutes or so it was necessary to halt to oil or

clean the cylinders, or to raise steam, or clear the charcoal out of the furnace ; then, perhaps, as soon as a fresh start had been made, the steam pressure would go down and down, until the vessel, instead of making headway, began to drift back with the current. The next trouble was that the *Stanley* ran ashore, knocked several holes in her side, and loosened or displaced a number of rivets. The engineers from all the steamers were called to the rescue ; but as they were compelled to work in a couple of feet of water, the repairs took some time, and it was not until the fourth day that the *Stanley* was able to continue her voyage.

Notwithstanding all these difficulties progress' was made, and on May 12th the expedition halted at Bolobo, where an abundant stock of provisions was obtainable. It was a good camping-place, and as many of the men showed signs of weakness Stanley decided to leave all who were out of condition to recruit for a while, under the charge of Ward and Bonny.

From Bangala, where the expedition arrived on May 30th, Tippu Tib departed direct for Stanley Falls ; while Stanley and the main body went on to Yambuya, the large settlement on the south bank of the Aruwimi, where Stanley had halted on his first visit to that river. Here he proposed to estab- lish a temporary depôt, under the charge of Bart- telot, who, with Jameson as his second in command,

was to remain in camp until the carriers promised
by Tippu Tib should arrive.   Stanley himself decided
to push on with an advance guard of the best men,
and the rear column was to follow at the earliest
possible date.

The Yambuya natives, though they abstained from
active hostilities, firmly refused to allow the expedition to land.   When several hours had been wasted
in fruitless negotiations, Stanley determined to carry
the thing through with a rush.   At a given signal
the men swarmed ashore, scrambled up the steep
bank, and made a dash for the village.   As the first
man landed the villagers fled, and by the time the
top of the bank was reached not a single native was
to be seen.   Closer inspection showed that the settlement consisted of many villages extending along the
river bank, and backed at a short distance by almost
impenetrable forest.   No time, however, was lost in
making unnecessary investigations, and as soon as
the men had taken up the quarters assigned to
them guards were set, and work began.

Among such surroundings it would have been the
height of imprudence to leave the depôt without
every possible protection, so, while some of the men
were told off to cut fuel for the steamers, which
were to return to Stanley Pool to fetch up the ammunition which had been stored there, the rest of
the force was detailed to build a stockade and cut
a ditch around the site of the proposed camp.   In

the course of a fortnight the intrenched camp was so far on the road to completion that Stanley felt justified in leaving Major Barttelot and Jameson to their own devices, and on the 28th of June the advance began. Lieutenant Stairs was seriously ill with fever, but though he was unable to walk he was so anxious to go forward that he was carried in a hammock.

Within a few yards of the camp the thick bush presented an apparently impenetrable front, and what was called by courtesy a path bore so little resemblance to anything that is usually so termed that it was constantly necessary to clear the way of tangled creepers, which stretched in all directions. Progress was necessarily slow, but late in the afternoon the leaders reached a point where the path opened out into a broad road, leading to a village called Yankonde. Each side of the road was marked by a stiff bush fence, so closely banked up as to be quite impassable, and at its farther end stood several hundred warriors with bow in hand, apparently daring the strangers to advance. The men halted, and it was then observed that the road fairly bristled with sharp-pointed pegs, smeared with poison, and set upright in the ground. Until these were removed, the road, for shoeless people, was absolutely impassable, and a dozen men were told off to pull up the pegs, while another dozen covered the workers with their rifles. Other parties were sent out to make their way through the bush behind the fences; but long before any one could reach the village the natives fired the huts, and after discharging a flight of arrows in the direction of the column, took to their heels. They did not, however, run far, and throughout the night they hovered round the camp, pouring in spears and arrows to the accompaniment of a chorus of unearthly yells. To guard against surprise a strong force of sentries was posted; but as it was useless to attempt firing in the dark, the orders for the night were merely to keep silence and a strict watch.

The first day's march was a fair sample of what continued for many weeks. Sometimes the way lay along a so-called track, where, however, it was constantly necessary to cut away dependent creepers. Sometimes there was no vestige of a track at all, and then the leaders, with their axes and billhooks, were compelled to clear every foot of ground to be traversed. Here and there giant trees crossed the route, forming barriers troublesome for the men and almost impassable for the donkeys; and in the neighbourhood of villages, where none of these hindrances existed, the ground was usually so liberally pegged that the greatest caution was necessary. Another danger lay in the various pitfalls and other traps for game which usually abounded in the vicinity of tracks and villages. With all these difficulties to overcome, travelling was necessarily slow and difficult, and in a six or seven hours' march it was very seldom that more than five miles were covered.

After a week of this sort of progress the expedition again touched the river, which presented a beautiful, calm stretch of water with no impediments to navigation. It occurred to Stanley that a great deal of trouble might be saved by launching the steel boat *Advance*, which hitherto had been carried in sections, and Jephson, who had special charge of the boat, was desired to fit the sections together. As soon as the boat was launched, Lieutenant Stairs, who was still too ill to walk, was put on board, and the rest of the available space was filled up with baggage. Near the river bank the bush was less thick than farther inland ; travelling was therefore decidedly more rapid, and on July 5th a village was reached. Its appearance was hailed with delight, for provisions were rapidly growing scarce, and for the last three days the men had been compelled to keep body and soul together on nothing better than a few manioc roots.

That evening, when the boat, which had been delayed by rapids, made its appearance, Jephson reported the discovery of a fleet of abandoned canoes. These he had secured to an island to await Stanley's pleasure, and he was forthwith sent back with additional men to bring a specially large one up to the camp. Above the village the river bank became more thickly inhabited—or it would be more correct

to say there were more villages, for in every case
the inhabitants appeared to have fled. This was
so far advantageous that the foragers were able to
obtain a plentiful supply of manioc and other vegetables entirely free of cost. The only drawback was
that nothing in the way of animal food was procurable, for whatever fowls or goats the natives might
have possessed had departed with their masters, and
the whole country was singularly devoid of game.

The greater part of July 11th was spent in the
navigation of a series of rapids which bordered the
deserted villages, and only a trifling advance was
made. During the whole time that the expedition
was in the neighbourhood not a single native was
seen, but on the 12th, as the column disappeared,
they were observed quietly stealing back with their
property.

Later in the day, when the boat was slowly
working its way up-stream, a native lad appeared
coming down with the current on a portion of
a broken canoe. As he approached the boat he
sprang aboard, and immediately making himself at
home, settled down to work, using his paddle with
good effect. His name, he said, was Bakula; and
though he was suspected of being a cannibal, he
proved himself a handy, useful lad, conforming
readily to the ways of his new friends, and supply-
ing them with a good deal of information respecting
the villages in the neighbourhood.

At this time several canoes were annexed, so that by July 16th the fleet consisted of the boat and five canoes. These were capable of carrying seventy-four men, and such a large quantity of goods that now half the land force was sufficient to carry what remained. This was, of course, a great relief to the porters, who were thus enabled on alternate days to march free of any load.

On the 17th rain fell so heavily and incessantly for several hours that it was impossible to go on, and equally impossible to find any comfort in camp. The sun-loving Africans, consequently, became extremely depressed, and it was not until some hours after the rain had ceased that they began to recover their usual cheerfulness. Their low spirits were possibly caused partly by increasing weakness, for it was now many days since they had had anything more sustaining than a vegetable diet. Better days, however, were coming; for on the 20th, when the expedition was in camp near a large settlement known as Mariri, some of the natives ventured up in a canoe, and, for the first time during the journey up the Aruwimi, consented to trade. On this occasion, it is true, only five fowls could be purchased; but a couple of days later Surgeon Parke captured a native woman, on whom he made such a favourable impression that she induced her neighbours to sell a considerable number of fowls. Prices were low in this neighbourhood, for a single cotton handkerchief would pay for a fowl; while rubbish, such as empty sardine, jam, or milk tins, could be readily exchanged for tobacco, sugar-cane, and maize. In appearance the people much resembled the natives of the Upper Congo country, and the salutation of peace—" *Seneenah* "—was the same word as that used by the natives of Manyuema, Uregga, and other districts beyond Stanley Falls. They were decidedly lighter-coloured than the Zanzibaris; and when in full dress, which consisted of a layer of red camwood powder mixed with oil, it was no easy matter to distinguish them from the red clay banks of the river.

On July 25th there was again a series of rapids to be negotiated, and the boats, with Jephson and Stanley in charge, struggled foot by foot up a dangerous channel between rocky islets and the bush-clad bank. While some of the men rowed, others endeavoured to assist them by clutching at the overhanging branches with hands and boat-hooks; but at almost the first touch of the bushes a swarm of furious wasps sallied out, and settled on hands, faces, necks—on every spot where there seemed to be a chance of planting a sting. With every muscle engaged in the fight with the waters, no one had a chance of beating off the infuriated insects. The only chance of getting rid of them was to hasten out of their neighbourhood; but with the rushing current, vicious pointed rocks, and swirling eddies, the battle was a hard one. Half maddened by the stings, however, the men gained new strength with every effort, and in less time than had seemed possible the "Wasp Rapids" were left astern.

CHAPTER XI.

TROUBLES IN THE FOREST.

EVERY difficulty passed seemed only to leave the way clear for some new misfortune. The stings of the wasps encountered at the rapids in many cases produced a sharp attack of fever; but a worse trouble, and one which affected the whole column, was the scarcity of food. It was reported that above the Wasp Rapids there was a long stretch of uninhabited country, where little or nothing eatable could be procured. It was therefore imperative that a supply of food should be laid in; but when the travellers attempted to barter, provisions were found to be at famine prices. A brass rod, twenty-eight inches long, only purchased three heads of Indian corn, four rods were the price of a fowl, and a cartridge pouch fetched a couple of plantains. As the trading proceeded several men were detected in the act of selling their cartridges; then tools began to go; and finally, in order that the camp might not be completely denuded, it became necessary to order off the natives. One of their principal men was seized as a hostage, and his friends were informed that, unless they traded fairly on the following day, the captive would be carried away, and the fields and gardens would be raided.

Morning came, and as there was no sign of the natives a party of foragers was ordered out, and in a few hours returned with an abundant supply of provisions. One difficulty was thus solved; but on August 1st, when the advance was resumed, one of the Zanzibari boatmen managed to capsize his canoe by careless steering. The result was the loss of a quantity of valuable beads and other property, including half a dozen rifles.

So far, notwithstanding the hardships of the route, not a single death had occurred since the column left Yambuya, but short commons, added to constant work in the damp dreariness of the forest, began to tell on both men and animals, and on August 2nd a man and a donkey died. Later that same day a large abandoned village was reached, and the men were proceeding to make themselves comfortable for the night, when the report went round that a dead body had been discovered in a hut. Shortly afterwards two or three others were found, and as it seemed pretty clear that the surviving inhabitants had been frightened away by the outbreak of some malignant disease, the intended camp was transferred to a healthier locality.

The native boy Bakula had had a good deal to

tell about some falls which he called Panga, where,
he said, the water fell from a height equal to that
of the tallest tree; and on August 4th the foot of
the cataract was reached. The actual fall was about
thirty feet in height, though at first sight it appeared
to be considerably greater, as for some distance
above the fall the water descended a steep slope.
A portage was unavoidable, so the boats were taken
out of the water, a road was cut, and three days
later the pioneers, with their boat and canoes, encamped at the head of the cataract. During this
time a foraging party had been busily engaged in
a search for provisions; but their endeavours were
not crowned with any marked success, though the
neighbourhood was comparatively thickly inhabited.
The natives were said to be cannibals, who did not
cultivate the land, but picked up any sort of living
they could, eating human flesh as a dainty, and at
other times feeding on snails, mushrooms, banana
stalks, fish, or roots.

Above this none too agreeable camp navigation
proved difficult and dangerous, owing to the strength
and swiftness of the current flowing down to the
cataract. A canoe was upset, but fortunately no
lives were lost, though, owing to the carelessness of
the Zanzibari crew, a couple of rifles and two cases
of gunpowder, which formed part of the cargo, went
to the bottom of the stream. At this part of the
river the construction of the villages completely

changed. Below Panga Falls most of the huts were
built with high conical roofs; but here they were
much lower, with low pitched roofs and strong log
palisades, which could easily be held against an in-
vading force, even if armed with rifles. The people,
too, were warlike and unapproachable; and on August 10th, when the foragers were out, one of them
was shot in the throat by a wooden arrow, which
was evidently poisoned, for though the wound did
not appear to be serious the poor fellow grew worse
and worse, and died of lockjaw a few days later.

A large settlement, called Avisibba, was reached
on August 13th. The river column was the first to
arrive, and the men encamped in a village situated
on the bank of a creek called the Ruku. It was a
prosperous-looking place, consisting of a wide, open
street bordered on each side by low palisaded huts,
beyond which grew a flourishing thicket of plaintains
backed by dense uncleared forest, where the villagers,
who had deserted their houses, lay in ambush to
attack the unwelcome strangers. All unsuspicious
of danger, the boats' crews, rifle in hand, searched
through the houses and plantain groves, and finding
them deserted gave no thought to the forest beyond.
The officers, too, were busy; for on the previous day
a Zanzibari had been shot near the camp, and it was
supposed that one of his comrades was guilty of the
murder. A court-martial was therefore summoned
to investigate the case; and while the inquiry was

in progress a party of men was detailed to cross the Ruku, with the view to foraging on the farther side. They had not been long gone when the court-martial was disturbed by sounds of firing; and as the land column had now arrived, Lieutenant Stairs, with a reinforcement of fifty men, hurried off to see what was the matter.

The court then resumed business, but as the firing continued the meeting was adjourned, and Stanley, with Dr. Parke, Captain Nelson, and a few men, hastened to the scene of action. As they approached a few flying arrows were seen, and Stairs met them with blood flowing fast from his chest. Parke at once took charge of him, and Stanley endeavoured to obtain some information, since, though his own men were firing volley after volley into the bushes on the farther side of the creek, not an enemy of any description was to be seen. It appeared that as the foragers attempted to cross the Ruku the villagers suddenly emerged from the farther side and sent a flight of arrows towards the boat. No one was hurt, but the men, alarmed at the sudden attack, paddled back to their own side of the creek and opened fire with their rifles. At this stage they were joined by Lieutenant Stairs, who had blazed away at the enemy until an arrow struck him and forced him to retire. Several men were also injured.

Scarcely had Stanley's informant finished his tale when a movement was seen on the farther bank,

and something was observed to be creeping from one
bush to another. It might be a man, and on the
chance that it was Stanley fired. Though he could
not see the result of his shot, a loud, wailing cry
told that his bullet had taken effect, and within two
minutes the shower of arrows completely ceased.
A guard was set to keep watch along the banks,
and the men were ordered into camp, though later
in the day another party went out in a different
direction, and succeeded in capturing seven goats.

The following morning two columns were dispatched to search for the antagonistic villagers, and
punish them for the unprovoked attack of the previous
day. It was not, however, very easy to find them;
and though their whereabouts was discovered, all
that the avenging columns could do was to fire at
random into the thick bush. The chief result was
the dispersal of the villagers, who retired farther into
the forest. The remainder of the day was spent in
foraging, and the next morning the march continued.

The last two days of the month were occupied in
the uncongenial task of portaging the boats past a
formidable cataract. The worst of the work had been
done, and a camping-place had been found, when
Stanley's servant raced up to his master, shouting at
the top of his voice that Emin Pasha had arrived.
Stanley could not believe the news, but the man
declared that Emin was coming in a canoe with the
Egyptian flag floating at the stern. Unable to doubt

further, Stanley dropped his work and rushed off in
headlong haste to the river bank. The news spread
through the camp, and the wildest excitement prevailed, when a sudden damper came, for the boat
which was supposed to be Emin's proved to be
manned by nine Manyuema, the servants of a slave
and ivory dealer called Ugarrowwa. His camp, it
was said, was about eight marches distant up-stream,
and there several hundred armed men were stationed.
An advance camp belonging to Ugarrowwa's party
was also said to be situated about six miles above
Stanley's halting-place, and to this belonged the
present visitors, who had been charged with the duty
of exploring the stream, to discover if Stanley Falls
could be reached by water. On this point Stanley
was able to give them all the information they required, so they decided to return to their camp, to
arrange, as they said, a proper reception for Stanley's
men when they should arrive on the following day.

Every one was highly delighted at the prospect of
reaching some sort of civilization, and shortly after
dawn preparations for the advance were made. The
six miles were covered in record time, but on arriving at the camp all was silent and deserted. The
dead bodies of a woman and a child, both evidently
murdered, lay on the ground; but the Manyuema
with their slaves had disappeared, and the explorers
could only suppose that they had been afraid of what
the white men might say or do on reaching a slave

camp. The Zanzibaris at least were bitterly disappointed. The damp, dark forest compared unfavourably with their own sunny land; they were sick of hard work and poor living; and five of them deserted that day, taking with them their loads of ammunition and salt. A day or two later five others deserted, with a miscellaneous assortment of ammunition, provisions, and clothing; and though a search-party was sent out to bring them back, only one man, one box of cartridges, and three rifles were recovered. So many desertions followed, that on September 4th it was found necessary to remove the springs of a number of the rifles, so as to render them useless, and thus deter several men known to be untrustworthy from deserting.

To reach Ugarrowwa's camp was now the immediate object in view, and day after day the weary travellers pushed forward, boating when possible, at other times clearing roads and dragging boats and canoes overland. But at last, on September 16th, during the midday halt, several shots were heard. Scouts were sent out, and in the course of an hour the welcome news was brought in that Ugarrowwa's camp was so close at hand that the chief himself would visit Stanley when the column halted for the night. By four o'clock the longed-for destination was safely reached, and the camp was pitched in the immediate neighbourhood of the traders' station.

No sooner had the expedition come to a halt than,

to the music of drums and the crashing of musketry, Ugarrowwa appeared in state, escorted by a whole fleet of canoes. The district in which his present camp was situated, he said, was called Bunda; but his followers had laid waste the whole neighbourhood, by way of retaliation for sundry outrages committed by the natives on various parties of ivory hunters. To the south-eastward the forest extended for hundreds of miles, rivers and lakes were few and far between, and during a journey extending over nine months he had only crossed one river before he reached the Ituri, as, at this part of its course, the Aruwimi was called.

His settlement approached more nearly to civilization than anything which had been seen on the Aruwimi. It was a large place, fortified with strong palisading, and in the centre the chief's house, strong enough to deserve the name of fort, was large and comfortable. Everything about the station betokened prosperity, and finding that Ugarrowwa was friendly disposed, Stanley arranged with him to leave the sick and disabled men under his charge until the rear column should arrive.

CHAPTER XII.

HARD TIMES.

ON September 19th Stanley, Jephson, Parke, and
Stairs, with all the men still in working
condition, again set out, leaving fifty-six invalids in
Ugarrowwa's charge. Heavy work lay ahead; food
became scarcer and scarcer; and in the course of
the next few marches rapid after rapid and cataract
after cataract made navigation almost impossible.
Foragers were sent out, but they met with little
success; and even on the rare occasions when plantains or bananas were found, the people were so
hungry that they consumed at a single meal an
amount of food which, with greater care and fore-
thought, might have kept them going for several days.

The 30th of September was a red-letter day, for
that morning Stanley discovered a native trap containing some fine fish, and Stairs lighted on an antelope caught in a pitfall. Later in the day a party
of Manyuema, who announced themselves as the followers of Kilonga-Longa, an Arab trader, who had a
station five days' journey up the river, made their

appearance. As the intervening country had been laid waste, and was entirely uninhabited, they advised Stanley to lay in a stock of provisions before proceeding farther. Good as the advice was, to carry it out proved impossible, since the neighbourhood of the camp was so poverty-stricken that the only thing procurable was a small supply of plantains. These were served out to the men, and on October 3rd the journey was continued, though at every mile navigation became more difficult.

Two days later a point was reached where, for canoes at least, the stream became absolutely impracticable. It was here joined by a tributary called the Ihuru, which flowed impetuously through a rocky gorge; while above the junction the Ituri descended a series of cataracts. That day no further advance was made. Though it was only a little more than a fortnight since the expedition left Ugarrowwa's station, work and privation had wrought terrible havoc. Several men had died, and of the two hundred and sixty-three who remained, fifty-two were utterly incapacitated by weakness and serious ulcers in the feet. Captain Nelson had also fallen a prey to this annoying complaint, and during the last few days he had become almost unable to walk. With so many cripples progress was necessarily very slow, and in a wilderness where food was unprocurable slow progress meant starvation for the whole party. This was apparent to Nelson, and he proposed that some of the Zanzibari headmen, who were really capable, intelligent fellows, should be sent ahead to Kilonga-Longa's station to obtain food for their famishing companions. The plan was so obviously good that the men were at once dispatched; and then, in the belief that to hasten forward with the bulk of the column would be to the advantage of all, Stanley decided to leave the cripples, and to push on as fast as possible with the rest of the men.

For nine days the poor fellows struggled forward, growing weaker and feebler at every step they took. Not a village, not even a hut, was to be seen on the river banks. The few provisions which they had brought with them were exhausted, and game was as scarce as human inhabitants. Once a small village was seen on an island; but when a party of foragers landed in the hope of obtaining supplies, all they could get was a small quantity of Indian corn and beans—barely enough to go round. Sometimes wild fruits were discovered; and on these, with forest beans—a somewhat peculiar vegetable which had to be carefully skinned and scraped before it was eaten—caterpillars, and grubs, the men managed to keep alive.

At last things looked so desperate that Stanley suggested sinking the boat, native fashion, in the stream, to be fetched on some future occasion; but to this Uledi, the coxswain, would not consent. If Stanley, he said, with the caravan, would push forward to Kilonga-Longa's settlement, he and his crew would remain with the boat, and, when they could not row, haul or pole her forward as best they could. In two or three days, if by that time he had not reached the settlement, he promised that he would send forward some men to overtake the column. To this unselfish plan every one agreed, and, relieved of the boat, the advance party was able to make somewhat better progress, until early in the morning of October 17th a jovial voice was heard singing in an unknown language. It was unlikely that natives would indulge in such noisy merriment, and it therefore seemed clear that at last Ipoto, the long-wished-for settlement, must have been reached. A rifle shot fired as a signal was answered by the discharge of several muskets, and the men pushed forward with renewed hope down the side of a valley, on the farther slope of which they saw crowds of people issuing from a prosperous-looking village.

Nothing could exceed the friendly kindness with which the Arabs welcomed their weary, footsore visitors. Kilonga-Longa himself was not at the station, but the headmen, Ismaili, Khamisi, and Sangaramini, had full authority in his absence. They allotted quarters to the pioneers, supplied them with provisions, and promised to send a relief party of eighty men to Nelson's camp. Everything seemed to be well, but on the third day a change came. Instead of the liberal supplies of food in which for the two previous days the men had revelled, a bare pittance of two ears of Indian corn per man was doled out; and even when Stanley promised to pay three times the current price for corn as soon as his rear column should arrive, nothing more could be obtained. Unfortunately, most of his best beads and cloth had been lost or stolen on the way, and the Arabs, seeing the comparatively valueless nature of his visible possessions, probably disbelieved in the existence of the alleged rear column with its rich and varied stores. However this might be, they refused to sell anything on credit; and the Zanzibaris, finding themselves famishing in the midst of plenty, began to trade away their rifles and ammunition, and even the very clothes on their backs. Yet the headmen, when questioned, denied all knowledge of the missing rifles. So, as the loss was too serious a menace to the success, indeed to the very existence of the expedition, to be passed over, the men were mustered, and those without arms were sentenced to be flogged.

A sense of fair play then induced another man to come forward and state that one of the condemned men was innocent, inasmuch as his rifle was at that moment in the possession of the speaker. He had seized it, he said, from one of the cooks named Juma, who was presumably the thief. On this Juma fled into hiding, but was subsequently captured, and being convicted of the theft of another rifle, was summarily hanged as an example to the rest. Rifles and ammunition, however, continued to disappear; and when Stanley remonstrated with Kilonga-Longa's Manyuema followers for receiving them, knowing them to be stolen, five were restored, and the sellers pointed out.

At that moment Uledi with his boat's crew appeared on the scene, with the good news that the boat was safe at the landing-place. Stanley then told him his tale of difficulties, and again Uledi came to the rescue, declaring that he could deal with the Manyuema, and bring them to a more friendly temper. This he succeeded in doing so effectually that not only did they apologize for their unkind behaviour, but made practical reparation in the shape of presents of corn.

Still the promised relief expedition had not been sent, and it was not until October 26th that Kilonga-Longa's headmen were induced to detail men to accompany Mr. Jephson and a party of Zanzibaris to Nelson's camp. When at last they started they made rapid progress, and in four days reached their destination—just in time not to be too late. Of the fifty-two men who had been left with Nelson only five still remained; and these, with Nelson himself, were rapidly approaching the last stages of famine. They had subsisted on herbs and fungi, eked out with a little wild fruit and a very few bananas brought in by a man named Umari, who, when Jephson reached the camp, was absent foraging with twenty-one men : the other twenty-five were dead, or had deserted. Nelson, though terribly weak, was in better health than when the expedition had left him ; and after a good meal or two he was able to begin the march to Ipoto, leaving Umari to follow on his return to the camp.

Stanley meanwhile had made blood brotherhood with Ismaili, and had arranged with him to board and lodge Nelson and the other sick, together with Surgeon Parke, who was to take charge of them until the rear column should arrive. He also engaged the services of guides to conduct the advance column to Ibwiri; and then, on October 28th, having provided to the best of his ability for the wellbeing of all, set out on the next stage of the march.

On November 10th, after a difficult journey along a route rendered at times almost impassable by huge piles of fallen timber, the district of Ibwiri was reached. Here there were five prosperous villages, rich in corn, plantains, bananas, potatoes, beans, sugar-cane, and melons. The natives, too, were friendly, and it was speedily arranged that the western portion of the clearing should be handed over to the expedition for as long as Stanley chose to halt. Jephson and his party had not yet over-taken the column; so, as the men all needed rest and refreshment, it was decided to camp for a while. This decision gave the greatest satisfaction to the half-starved Zanzibaris, who now, almost for the first time for months, were able thoroughly to satisfy their hunger.

Jephson appeared on November 16th, bringing an account of affairs at Ipoto which was anything but encouraging. Notwithstanding the fact that Ismaili had made brotherhood with Stanley, no sooner had the latter departed than the Manyuema headman began systematically to ill treat and half famish the convalescents who had been left in his charge. The only thing to be said in his favour was that he had omitted to exact any particular concessions, and recognizing this, Stanley abstained from expressing his real opinions to the Manyuema guides who had accompanied him. All he could do was to send a letter to Nelson, and when the guides departed on the day following Jephson's arrival he parted from them in a friendly way.

His connection with them had been a doubtful benefit throughout, though his opportune arrival at their village had doubtless saved the lives of many of his men. But their numerous raids had earned the ill-will of every native who had heard the name of Manyuema, and it now appeared that this dislike was extended to every one who had ever been connected with them. In every district and at every village the people were ready to take up arms against the expedition ; and though the Ibwiri had at first been friendly, they were now prepared to commence hostilities.

During the next few days reconnoitring parties
were sent out, and on November 21st Stairs reported
the discovery of a good path running to the eastward.
This was encouraging news, and the men, most of
whom had fully recovered their strength, became
anxious to resume the journey. A few of them
might have been all the better for a longer rest, but
as no one was really incapable camp was broken
up on the 24th, and after two days' marching the
watershed between the Ihuru and Ituri rivers was
reached. Beyond this lay the district of Indenduru,
where every tree and plant was covered with dripping
moss, and at every mile or so a stream had to be
crossed. In this district a day's halt was made with
the view of reconnoitring, and a suitable path having
been discovered, the march was continued on the
29th. The next day a woman was captured, and
induced to act as guide through a clearing rendered
almost impracticable by the numerous fallen trees
which crossed one another in every direction. Beyond this the ground sloped gently upward, and
following a well-trodden pathway the pioneers
speedily reached the top of the slope.

Here a glorious view stretched away before them.
To the eastward, whither the travellers were bound,
was beautiful, open country, well grassed and inter-
spersed with stretches of woodland, rocky hills, and
pleasant valleys. To the eastward, too, lay a mountain peak to which Stanley at once gave the name

of Pisgah, because from its neighbourhood he had
obtained the first glimpse of the fertile country.
Several days, however, passed before the travellers
were really clear of the forest; and it was not until
December 4th that, soon after crossing a narrow
stream, which an old woman, captured in the neighbourhood, called the Ituri, the men finally emerged
from the forest. Before them lay mile after mile of
beautiful, undulating grass-land, and the next day
they reached the fertile district of Mbiri, where in-
numerable cone-shaped huts were scattered broad-
cast among banana groves. In this region good
paths seemed to run in every direction, and rapid
progress was made. The only drawback now was the
unfriendliness of the natives, by whom that evening
the camp was attacked. A few volleys, however,
cleared off the assailants, and the rest of the night
passed quietly. On the following day another river,
also called by the natives Ituri, was crossed; and as
a third stream was also known by this name, Stanley
came to the conclusion that not only the main river
but also its tributaries shared the appellation.

Beyond this last river, which, by way of distin-
guishing it, Stanley termed the East Ituri, lay a
well-cultivated district, rich in every description of
agricultural products. Passing through this the
travellers reached a mountainous district called Mazamboni's Range. The country was delightful; but
the inhabitants were less charming, for as the column

passed down a pleasant, fruitful valley war-cries sounded from above, and the hill-tops were seen to be well sprinkled with warriors. They evidently intended to fight; but camping time was at hand, and an isolated flat-topped kopje, conveniently situated in the immediate neighbourhood, offered a secure resting-place for the night. It was a place which a few riflemen could easily defend against any number of men unprovided with firearms; so, while a few men were told off to act as sentries, the rest cut brushwood for a zeriba, fetched water, and piled the brushwood into an impassable fence.

The opposing force had nearly trebled its numbers, but though some of the bowmen advanced against the camp, two or three volleys from the summit caused them to retire to a safe distance. In the morning, however, hostile demonstrations were resumed, and war-cries echoing through the valley clearly showed the mind of the population. Stanley, however, had no wish to fight, and finding that one of his men understood the language, he directed him to try to bring the natives to a more peaceful frame of mind. A long parley resulted in a suspension of hostilities; and later in the day the chief, Mazamboni, sent word to say that he would like to see samples of the white man's goods. Some scarlet cloth and brass rods were given to the messengers, who then departed, after giving Stanley to understand that Mazamboni himself would visit the camp on the following day to make brotherhood with the white men.

Before morning the natives once more changed their minds. Instead of desiring peace they now again declared for war; and it was not until three companies of riflemen, commanded respectively by Stairs, Jephson, and Uledi, had scoured the neighbourhood and burned a number of villages that they were finally reduced to order. On the following day Mazamboni sent an envoy, who announced that, though the chief himself had wished for peace, his young men had insisted on making war on the strangers. But now many of them had been killed, and the others were willing to make peace. Stanley replied that he was quite ready to do so, and supposing, therefore, that hostilities were at an end, he gave orders for the advance. Early on the following morning the camp was broken up, and the expedition passed on its way through a series of ravines and valleys.

But again the natives were on the war-path, and they hovered round, annoying the column, until at last the explorers, goaded to desperation, turned upon them and burned every hut in the vicinity. After this they were allowed to proceed in peace, and the next day's march brought them to the edge of a tableland, whence they looked down on the blue waters of the Albert Nyanza.

CHAPTER XIII.

FORT BODO.

THE vast Congo basin now lay to the rearward, for the ridge on which the camp was situated divided the streams which join the Congo from those which, emptying themselves into the Albert Nyanza, belong to the Nile system. To the lake the descent was long and steep; for, while the camp was perched about five thousand feet above sea-level, the altitude of the Albert Nyanza is only two thousand four hundred feet. In any circumstances, to scramble down such a place would have been no easy task for heavily-laden men; and now the difficulties were increased by the hostility of the natives, who harassed the rear guard by hanging round the track, jeering at the men, and at every opportunity pouring in a shower of arrows. Owing partly, no doubt, to the roughness of the ground, and partly to the smartness of the rifle fire with which every flight of arrows was answered, very little damage was done. But the natives would not relinquish the attack, and every few minutes it was necessary to halt and drive them

back. Thus the descent occupied about three hours ;
and even when the force was snugly encamped in an
almost impregnable spot on the farther side of a
stream the natives did not relinquish hostilities. A
determined night attack was, however, successfully
repulsed, and in the morning the column was
allowed to march peacefully down to the lake shore.

Here the inhabitants, though not aggressive, had
no welcome for the strangers; and at the village of
a chief named Katonza the people repelled every
attempt to make friends, and flatly refused to trade,
or even to accept presents. The utmost they could
be induced to do was to point out the path along the
lake shore to the northward, where, as they said,
they had heard that strange people were encamped.
But though they had heard that a white man—probably Emin Pasha's coadjutor and friend, Captain
Casati—was in Unyoro on the farther side of the
lake, of Emin himself they had nothing to say.
His very name seemed to be unknown; and after
marching up the shore as far as the island of Kasenya
without obtaining any news, it was unanimously
decided to return to Ibwiri and there form a station,
where the bulk of the expedition might remain with
the baggage, while a flying column hastened back to
Ipoto and Ugarrowwa's to fetch the convalescents,
the boat, and a fresh supply of ammunition.

No other course, indeed, was open, for though
Wadelai, where Emin was supposed to be encamped,

was only four days' distance by water, without canoes the lake could not be navigated. That these could not be bought had already been ascertained; that they could not be built was equally clear, for the barren shores of the lake did not produce a single tree suitable for the purpose. Of course a land route might be taken, but the march could not be made under twenty-five days : food was scarce, and the natives probably hostile. Five cases of cartridges had been expended during the recent fighting; and though forty-seven cases remained, further hostilities at the same rate would so reduce the stock that what was left could be of little use either to Emin or his would-be rescuers.

To remain at the lake would only be to waste time and run the risk of famine, so on the morning of December 16th the return journey began. It was no light task to scramble up the two thousand feet of steep, rocky slope which lay between the lake and the tableland above, especially as the natives hung on the line of march, and succeeded in cutting off three stragglers. A few sharpshooters, however, turned out to avenge their comrades, and the good practice which they made with their rifles taught the assailants to keep their distance. Thenceforward the march was comparatively uneventful, and on January 7, 1888, Ibwiri was safely reached.

Expectations had been entertained of camping comfortably in the village of a chief named Boryo, with whom Stanley had already made acquaintance; but alas for these fond hopes! In accord with what seemed to be a universal custom in that district, the village, having been contaminated by the presence of strangers, had been burned; but the best planks, together with the supplies of corn, had been stored in the forest. These were forthwith annexed, and that same day all hands set to work on the construction of a fort, to which the name of Bodo—that is, Peaceful—was given. By the 18th of January such good progress had been made that Lieutenant Stairs, who was to take charge of the flying column, received his marching orders.

While Stairs, with ninety-seven coloured men of various grades, made his way westward, the rest of the force, numbering seventy all told, completed the fort, and cleared several acres of land around it. Then prowling natives were detected in the neighbourhood, and as they were obviously bent on mischief scouts were detailed to rout them. It then appeared that several parties of dwarfs were encamped within a mile radius of the fort. As long as they remained no security could be expected, so the camps were destroyed, and the pygmies hunted into the recesses of the forest.

No sooner were the dwarfs disposed of than a new annoyance turned up in the shape of an overwhelming incursion of rats, fleas, and mosquitoes. The rats, though they raided the corn, were comparatively

innocuous; but the same could not be said of the
mosquitoes, which were only kept at bay by suffocat-
ingly close mosquito curtains of thick muslin, while
the fleas swarmed to such an extent that the floors
had to be damped constantly and swept twice daily.
Then came armies of red ants, which overran the
whole place, and drove the lightly-clad Zanzibaris
half mad with their venomous bites.

On February 8th the Egyptian flag was hoisted,
and a salute of twenty-one rounds was fired in its
honour. Scarcely had the echoes died away in the
forest when a shout from one of the sentries announced the arrival of visitors, and in a few moments
Surgeon Parke strode in. His bronzed, healthy
appearance and active gait contrasted strongly with
the feeble appearance of Captain Nelson, who was
still troubled with ulcers in the feet. Most of the
men, too, seemed weak and ill, and wore a famished
look, which told only too plainly how badly the
Manyuema had fulfilled their promises. They had,
indeed, utterly ignored the arrangement made with
Stanley. No sooner was his back turned than they
began systematically to ill treat the sick; and though
Parke called their attention to the agreement signed
by the three headmen, they provided less and less
food, until finally, for seven weeks, the supply ceased
entirely. The excuse pleaded was scarcity : evidently
the idea was to compel the half-famished people to
sell their rifles and ammunition, for it was observed

that, though no food could be obtained on the terms
mentioned in the agreement, for " cash down " provisions were always forthcoming.   To make matters
worse, the filthy habits of the Manyuema speedily
converted the camp into a hotbed of disease.   Both
Nelson and Parke were confined to their beds for
weeks by sickness ; and finally, when Kilonga-Longa,
with a force of about four hundred people, arrived at
the station, the talked-of scarcity became a reality.
The Manyuema were compelled to search far and
near for food, and when Stairs appeared on the
scene, twelve of the Zanzibaris were absent with one
of the foraging parties.

Four days after the arrival of Parke and Nelson
the boat sections were brought in by Stairs and
his men.   The expedition was thus restored to a
condition in which it could travel anywhere ; and
Stanley had now to decide between the rival claims
of his own rear column on the one hand and those
of Emin Pasha on the other.   Whether to return to
help Barttelot or to advance to relieve Emin was the
question which had to be answered; and as the
result of a council held on the evening of Stairs's
arrival it was agreed that, while the bulk of the force
went on in search of Emin, a smaller party should
return to meet Barttelot.   For the latter duty volunteers were asked to come forward ; and finally, out
of fifty Zanzibaris who offered themselves, twenty
fine capable fellows were selected.   It was further

agreed that Stairs should accompany them to Ugarrowwa's; and then, having seen the relief party
safely across the river, should return to Fort Bodo,
bringing with him the men who had been left at
Ugarrowwa's in September. Meanwhile the bulk
of the force was to remain at Fort Bodo until the
end of March, so as to give Stairs a chance of taking
part in the long-talked-of " relief of Emin."

On February 19th, two days after Stairs's departure for Ugarrowwa's, Stanley developed an attack
of internal inflammation, which, combined with an
abscess in the arm, kept him on the sick list for
several days. Meanwhile the recently planted corn
was growing with wonderful rapidity, and Nelson
and Stanley, the two convalescents, amused themselves by watching its progress. Evidently there need
be no fear of famine in the fort; for by the end of
March the corn was in ear, and had reached such a
height that an elephant could have concealed himself in it. To Nelson, after his long experience of
scarcity, the sight must have been specially grati-
fying; for it was now arranged that he, with all the
sick or weakly men, should remain in garrison at
Fort Bodo, while Stanley, with Parke, Jephson, and
a hundred and twenty-six men, conveyed the boat
to the Nyanza.

On April 2nd the march began. The journey
through a twice-traversed region was comparatively
uneventful, and a twelve days' journey brought the

party to Mazamboni's country. This time all was peace and harmony; and when, after a little coy hesitation, the natives ventured into the camp, Stanley inquired if they had ever heard of a white chief who many moons ago was said to have lived near the Nyanza. The answer was entirely satisfactory. Yes, they had heard of him; and only two moons after Bula Matari left their country a white man named Malleju (the Bearded One) came to Katonza's village in a big iron canoe. He had gone away again; but, said Mazamboni, his runners should go to the lake forthwith, and tell Katonza that Malleju's white brother had arrived. Evidently Emin was safe; but this being the case, why had he not sent his " iron canoe " down the lake to meet the relief force which he knew was due to arrive on or about December 15th. Of course it was possible that the news of the dispatch of the expedition had failed to reach him; but no amount of guessing could solve the riddle until Emin himself supplied the answer. At all events the column might rest quietly for a day, and April 14th was spent in a palaver which lasted for hours, and only ended when Mazamboni had made blood brotherhood with Jephson.

Two days later similar ceremonies took place at the village of Mpinga, chief of the Bavira tribe, an agricultural race, who for some reason were held in contempt by their neighbours, the cattle-rearing

Wahuma, of whom Mazamboni was chief. The two races lived in peace, and traded together; but they never intermarried, nor would a Mhuma (the singular form of Wahuma) take up his residence in a Bavira village.

From Mpinga's village the column went on to the Kavalli district, of which Mbiassa, a good-looking young Mhuma, was chief; and here Stanley received a letter which Emin had left with the lake shore natives, who in turn had handed it on to Mbiassa. In this epistle Emin requested Stanley to stay where-ever he might happen to be when he received the letter, and to send Emin word of his whereabouts. On receipt of his message Emin would come down to Nyamsassi, a lake island at no great distance from Kavalli, and they could there meet and arrange their plans. In accordance with this request Jephson was entrusted with the task of communicating with Emin, while Surgeon Parke and thirty-five men were detailed to act as escort to the Nyanza, and assist Jephson and his crew to launch the boat.

All went satisfactorily; and so well did Stanley and Emin time their journeys, that on April 29th they reached the rendezvous within a few hours of each other. On the following day the camp was removed to Nsabe, a pleasant grassy spot about three miles north of Nyamsassi Island, and there the expedition halted quietly until May 24th. The time was occupied by Stanley in long discussions with Emin, before whom he laid three propositions :—

1. That he and his men should return to Egypt, where it was probable, though not certain, that Emin would obtain further employment.

2. That Emin should transfer his services to the Congo Free State, where King Leopold offered him the post of governor, with a salary of £1,500 per annum. In the event of his accepting this offer, his duty would be to maintain order in the Equatorial Provinces virtually abandoned by Egypt, and keep open the line of communication between the Congo and the Nile.

3. That Emin, with such of his troops as chose to accompany him, should retire to the north-east corner of the Victoria Nyanza, whither the relief force would escort him and see him settled before proceeding to Zanzibar to obtain the sanction of the East African Association. This sanction, it is true, had not been guaranteed; but Stanley had no doubt that the Association would rejoice to obtain the services of so excellent an administrator as Emin.

To the two first propositions Emin returned an unqualified negative, but the third was more to his liking; and after much discussion it was arranged that Jephson and four men should remain with him, while Stanley returned to bring up the rear column.

CHAPTER XIV.

FROM THE NYANZA TO BANALYA.

SHORTLY after six o'clock on the morning of May 24th Stanley's force marched out of camp, and proceeded to Badzwa village, obtaining on the way a view of a snow-clad mountain, supposed by the men to be composed of salt. At first it resembled a silvery cloud; but as the outline revealed itself more clearly, Stanley saw that he was gazing on a vast mountain mass, and guessed that it must be a summit of the hitherto unvisited and unknown range called by the natives Ruwenzori—" the Cloud King." It was a grand discovery, for no previous white explorer of the lake had seen the mountain, and no one had credited the neighbourhood of the Nyanza with the possession of a mountain rising above the limit of eternal snow. As, however, the mountain lay some seventy miles south of the line of march, for the present, at least, time and circumstances did not allow the discoverer the luxury of a closer view of Ruwenzori.

At Badzwa news was received that two powerful

chiefs, named Kadongo and Musiri, had combined
together to attack the column on the road between
Mpinga's and Mazamboni's villages. This, if true,
was serious; for though Emin had reinforced the
expedition with about a hundred carriers of the
Madi tribe, there were only a hundred and eleven
rifles, and ammunition was very scarce. To beat off
a determined assault would be difficult, if not impossible; so, instead of waiting to be attacked, Stanley
determined to be beforehand with the chiefs. Forty
Zanzibaris, under two of their own headmen, were
detailed to carry Kadongo's camp by storm; and
this they successfully did, though Kadongo himself
saved his life by shouting to the assailants that he
was Bula Matari's friend.

On the return of the victorious Zanzibaris the
march was resumed. Scarcely had a start been made
when Mazamboni's brother, Katto, made his appearance with a party of Wahuma bearing a red flag.
Stanley informed the chief of the expected attack, and
requested him to make all speed back to Mazamboni,
and ask for assistance in an attack on Musiri, which
Stanley proposed to make at dawn on the next
morning but one. Katto replied that time was
short, but he thought the thing could be accomplished, and he hastened back to Mazamboni, while
Stanley went to solicit the aid of Mpinga and his
Bavira.

Mpinga readily agreed, and on May 29th the allies

set out at three o'clock in the morning, Mazamboni's men leading the way, while Mpinga's brought up the rear. By six o'clock Usiri, Musiri's country, was reached; but as Stanley's warriors streamed over the land they found it utterly deserted, for Musiri, having got wind of the intended attack, had judiciously removed his people and live stock to some safe locality. Men, women, children, cattle, goats, and fowls had all disappeared, and nothing remained to be seized by the victors but a plentiful supply of corn, tobacco, and vegetables. The result, though possibly disappointing to the allies, was highly satisfactory to Stanley, who thus gained his object of clearing the road without the expenditure of a single cartridge.

The road was now open, and on June 8th the columns marched safely into Fort Bodo, where Stanley was greeted by Stairs, whose journey to Ugarrowwa's and back had occupied seventy-one days instead of the thirty-nine estimated by Stanley. This unexpected delay was due first to an attempt to make use of native paths, which, though they seemed to run in the right direction, eventually led the travellers so far from their route that they were compelled to retrace their steps. Then heavy and constant rains caused Stairs to suffer so severely from fever that on reaching Ugarrowwa's he was compelled to keep his bed for two days. Nor were these all his difficulties. Nearly half the men left in Ugarrowwa's charge had died, and the remainder were still so weak and ill that, as Stairs perceived, seven of them could only undertake the march at the gravest risk of their lives.

Ugarrowwa, however, flatly refused to keep them longer, and on March 18th Stairs, with his convoy of invalids, set out for Fort Bodo. Heavy rains again added to the difficulties of the march, and greatly increased the sufferings of the invalids, only fourteen of whom lived to reach the fort. Stairs himself had severe daily attacks of fever, and constant wettings had terribly depressing effects on all the men. Consequently, when at last the fort was reached, so few of the party were fit for further exertion that Stairs was unwillingly obliged to abandon his long-cherished intention of following the column to the Nyanza.

About a week was spent by Stanley in making arrangements and preparations for the march through the forest, and also for the safety of Fort Bodo and its garrison during the absence of the main column. The fort was by this time in so good a state for defence that Stanley had no scruple about leaving a small force under the command of Lieutenant Stairs, who, with Nelson and Parke, was to remain in charge of the depôt, while Stanley, with a party of volunteers, went to the assistance of the rear column. It was impossible to say when he might return, but that he could not reach Fort Bodo before the end of the year was certain. It was probable that Emin Pasha and

Jephson might come up about the middle of August, and Stanley recommended that, in the event of their bringing a sufficient force of carriers to remove the goods, the garrison should return with them to the lake; otherwise Stairs was to remain at the fort until the arrival of the rear column.

Early on June 16th Stanley and his men—a little over two hundred in all, including ninety-five Madi porters—marched out of Fort Bodo. Long experience of forest travelling had taught them what difficulties to expect; and though the skewers, the swamps, the ants, the creepers, the fallen logs, the tree-encumbered clearings, and all the other obstacles that on the former journey had caused so many delays, still obstructed the path, good progress was made. So rapid, indeed, was the advance that on June 28th the column reached Nelson's "Starvation Camp" at the mouth of the Ihuru tributary. So far all had gone well; but now the Madis, who, out of sheer laziness, had wasted their stock of food, began to suffer from hunger. Their untaught minds were unable to comprehend that before them lay a region where for many days no food could be obtained; and finding their loads heavy, they had purposely thrown away part of their corn. Thus, shortly after Starvation Camp had been left behind, their strength faltered, they lagged sadly, and when, on July 7th, the column was overtaken by a heavy shower, three of the Madis, unable in their weakened state to withstand the cold and wetting, fell dead in their tracks. After this men died almost daily; and though occasional plantations of bananas or plantains were discovered, the supply never equalled the demand.

To make matters worse, Ugarrowwa's camp, which was reached on July 13th, was found to be deserted. Evidently the Arabs had been driven away by famine, for the ground was strewn with skeletons, and nothing eatable was to be found in the neighbourhood. The Zanzibaris, however, foraged diligently, but though some plantains were found, the quantity was limited; and as the column pressed forward the skeletons which here and there lay by the wayside proved that Ugarrowwa's people had fallen on hard times. Thanks to their own incurable improvidence, the luckless Madis suffered even more severely, and day by day one or more lay down and died of sheer weakness and hunger. Disease, too, broke out among them, and by the end of July those who still survived were in a truly deplorable condition. They were quite unfit to march, and it was a great relief when some canoes were found in which the sick and baggage could be embarked.

A few days later (August 10th) Ugarrowwa was overtaken just above Wasp Rapids, where he had arrived on the previous day. With him, to Stanley's great surprise, were the survivors of the Zanzibaris who, nearly six months before, had left Fort Bodo to communicate with Major Barttelot. The poor fellows had a sad tale to tell. At first all had gone well with them, and they had reached Avisibba without mishap; but there troubles began, and shortly after that village was passed several men were hurt, more or less seriously, by arrows. Still they pushed on, but below Panga Falls the journey became a sort of running fight. Neither by night nor by day were they allowed a moment's peace, and by the time Wasp Rapids were reached only eleven men remained unhurt. Here a most determined attack was made by an almost overwhelming force, but the plucky Zanzibaris succeeded in driving off their assailants. Then, having fortified their camp and posted sentries, they prepared to pass the night.

But worn out as they were with incessant work and worry the sentries fell asleep. This was the natives' opportunity. Rendered bold by the darkness and silence they rushed the camp, and the sleeping Zanzibaris were aroused to a knowledge of their danger by the wild shrieks of one of their number who was stabbed as he lay. Fortunately, it was not yet too late for defence, and again and again the Zanzibaris fired their rifles into the dark mass crowding upon them. Many of the natives fell, and at last, just as the ammunition began to fail, the survivors took to their heels. Two of the Zanzibaris had been killed, and a third, who was mortally wounded, with his last breath advised his comrades to return to Ugarrowwa's. Only four men were now uninjured, and in the morning, when they took counsel together, it was unanimously decided that the advice of the dying man should be followed.

Then the retreat began; but still the natives hung around, and attacked at every opportunity. At Panga Falls another man was killed; and when Ugarrowwa's village was reached, fifteen out of the sixteen survivors were wounded. Their bravery had touched the somewhat hard heart of Ugarrowwa. He took every care of them, and by the time Stanley came up thirteen of the wounded had completely recovered. The other two were still ailing, and one of them eventually died.

Ugarrowwa now presented Stanley with three large canoes, which, added to those he already possessed, afforded accommodation for all the men. Rapid progress was therefore made, and early on August 17th the flotilla approached Banalya, which, when last seen, was a prosperous, thickly-inhabited district. But for many miles the canoes had been passing between silent and deserted banks; every village had been abandoned, and not a sign of life was visible. Banalya at first presented no variation of the rule, and it therefore came rather as a surprise when, about half-past nine in the morning, a stockaded village was observed in the distance. Formerly no such thing had existed in the neighbourhood; for the people of Banalya, secure in their own strength, had scorned to make use of any kind of fortification. What could it mean ?

Then white-clad people were descried, and in a few moments, as Stanley watched the village through his glass, a red flag, displaying the well-known crescent and star of the Egyptian standard, was hoisted. Then the truth burst upon him—it was the long-wished-for camp of the rear column, and a shout from the men gathered on the bank to watch the approaching canoes assured him beyond any possibility of doubt that he had verily and indeed reached his goal. A few moments later he was shaking hands with Mr. Bonny, who, on hearing of his arrival, had hurried out to meet him. But where were the others ?

It was a sad tale that Bonny had to tell, for of all the Europeans whom Stanley had left at Yambuya Bonny alone remained. The major was dead, Troup invalided home, Ward was at Bangala, and Jameson had gone to Stanley Falls in the hope of obtaining porters from Tippu Tib. That misfortune of some sort had overtaken the rear column was only too evident. But the full story of trouble had yet to be told.

CHAPTER XV.

THE REAR COLUMN.

WHEN Stanley, with the advance column, began the long and difficult journey up the Aruwimi on June 28, 1887, the only Europeans left in charge at Yambuya were Major Barttelot and Mr. Jameson. These two had their hands quite full; for there was a boma or bush fence round the camp to be completed, a deep ditch to be dug, and firewood for the steamer *Stanley* to be cut, not to mention sundry odds and ends of work, all of which required attention. They soon found that incessant personal supervision must be the order of the day, for the men were not by any means disposed to over-exert themselves, and stopped work directly they were left to their own devices. At night the case was as bad as by day, for the sentries who were posted to guard the camp took every opportunity of going to sleep, and before they could be cured of this dangerous habit it was found necessary to inflict several severe thrashings.

Another trouble which began to make itself felt

immediately after Stanley's departure was scarcity of food. Manioc and bananas, the principal native products, were indeed procurable; but no game of any description existed in the neighbourhood, and the natives, most of whom had removed from the immediate locality, were unwilling or unable to supply fowls or goats. Of the European provisions served out by Stanley to the two officers, the amount was almost ridiculously small: two and a half pounds of coffee, one and a half pounds of tea, half a pound of sugar, three tins each of jam and butter, one tin of salt, one tin of flour, four tins of condensed milk, two tins of biscuits, and half a tin each of red herrings, tapioca, chocolate, and sago, with a few other trifles, composed the six months' ration given out to each man. Occasionally a fish or two or a small fowl were obtained, and these made a welcome change; but as a general rule, Barttelot and Jameson were forced to content themselves with a meagre diet of boiled rice and beans.

The men, whose principal diet was manioc, fared even worse, and illness soon broke out in the camp. The first death occurred on July 1st, when one of the Zanzibaris, who had been ill for some time, breathed his last. So far neither of the Englishmen had been seriously ill, but both had been out of sorts, and the major, who suffered from what appeared to be some sort of low fever, became unable to eat the rough fare available.

At last, despairing of obtaining meat by ordinary means, Jameson decided to capture one or two native women, in the hope of inducing their friends to ransom them with goats or fowls. With this end in view, he and a few of the men lay in wait by one of the manioc plantations, and soon succeeded in catching a boy, two women, and a baby, all of whom were led off in triumph to the camp. There Barttelot presented the boy with four brass rods, and sent him off to tell the chief of his tribe that the women would be given up in return for a supply of goats and fowls. Shortly afterwards the husband of the woman with the baby made his appearance, and offered five goats and ten fowls as a ransom. He was informed that for double that number of goats and fowls both women would be released, and that a further contribution of honey would ransom the baby; but until these were brought in, the captives must remain in the camp. He therefore departed, promising to return in the morning; and this he did, bringing one fowl and some fish. In consideration of this he was allowed to see his wife; and thus negotiations continued for some days, during which several more fowls were brought in.

Thus, with plenty of work and worry, and very little interest or excitement, July wore away. On August 4th a rumour reached the camp that Tippu Tib's people were coming down the Aruwimi in canoes, and had burned a village, in spite of being assured that the chief was Bula Matari's brother. This was puzzling, for, as Tippu Tib had for some time been established at Stanley Falls, what could his canoes be doing on the Aruwimi? Four or five days later the mystery was explained, for the raiders turned out to be a band of marauding Arabs, who were coming down the Aruwimi, and destroying every village they found.

On August 12th one of the deserters from Stanley's column limped into camp, bringing rather a pitiful account of the hard times on which the column had fallen. Food had run short, the men were fast weakening, several had fallen ill, and one had been injured in a skirmish with the natives. The prospect was not encouraging; but on the 14th the arrival of the *Stanley*, with Ward, Troup, and Bonny, the stores, and a number of Zanzibaris on board, gave a wonderful fillip to the two weary officers. After the departure of the *Stanley* down-stream camp life settled into a regular routine, and Barttelot and Jameson were relieved of some work, as now the five Englishmen took it in turn to act as orderly officer. At half-past five in the morning the big native drum aroused the sleepers, and at six the men were told off for their respective duties, such as standing sentry, sweeping the camp, cutting wood, and collecting manioc. Noon brought dinner and a couple of hours' rest, and then work was resumed until half-past five. At sunset additional sentries were posted, and the duties of the orderly officer of the day included the not very pleasant task of making the round of the sentries three times during the night. To these duties Bonny added the important charge of catering, while to Ward the arrangements for the officers' mess were entrusted.

On August 18th ten of Tippu Tib's men were brought in by a reconnoitring party of Zanzibaris. They said that they had been sent from the Falls to collect men, and that seven hundred porters who also started with them had come across one of Stanley's camps, and had therefore leaped to the conclusion that the whole force had gone forward, consequently they had returned to Tippu Tib. This might be true, but also it might not; and on August 23rd, Jameson and Ward set out for the Falls to learn the real state of affairs. Nothing very satisfactory could, however, be discovered. Tippu Tib and his people were keeping the Mohammedan festival answering to Christmas, and though Tippu Tib made many promises to collect men, Jameson and Ward had to return to Yambuya without receiving anything more satisfactory than empty words.

Slowly the days passed until the end of September. No porters had arrived, and now came news which destroyed the last lingering hope that the rear column might overtake Stanley. Tippu Tib, ashamed, as he said, to come himself, sent word that he was unable to supply the promised men. Rumours of the heavy work of the expedition had reached his camp, and his followers, being apparently not altogether under control, had scattered themselves over the country on their usual business of fighting, raiding, and trading. Forty carriers, of whom Barttelot might dispose as he would, were all he could then supply; but he had sent to Kassongo for a reinforcement, which, however, could not reach Stanley Falls for about another month. By this reckoning some porters might arrive at Yambuya in six weeks' time. Without them it was impossible to advance the baggage; and the officers could not blind themselves to the fact that their chance of going forward was daily diminishing. Indeed, on Stanley's reckoning, it was not improbable that by the time the rear column was in a condition to move, the advance column would have returned from the Nyanza.

Slowly and sadly the days dragged along. The six weeks came to an end without bringing a sign of the reinforcement, and almost the only events which distinguished one day from another were the illness of one or other of the officers and the frequent deaths among the men, of whom by the end of the year no less than forty-one had been laid in the camp graveyard.

The New Year (1888) brought no brighter prospects, and by February 5th the number of deaths had risen to fifty. Some of the men had been ill for weeks, and were so reduced in strength that after a cold wet day or night one or two of them almost invariably died. It was distressing work, for in the absence of proper medicines Bonny, with his limited medical knowledge, could do little or nothing to save the poor fellows who died, as it seemed, of no specific disease. The trouble doubtless lay with the manioc, of which there are two varieties. One kind is wholesome and edible either raw or cooked; but the other, or bitter variety, which grew at Yambuya, though wholesome enough when properly prepared by long steeping in water and thorough cooking, in its raw condition is slow but deadly poison. This, apparently, was unknown to officers and men; and the poor fellows, whom a little more knowledge would have saved, went on day after day ignorantly eating the bitter manioc in its raw state or insufficiently cooked and unsoaked. The fact that very little manioc was eaten by the officers, who lived chiefly on rice and beans, doubtless accounted for their immunity from the unknown complaint that killed so many men.

On February 14th, Major Barttelot and Mr. Jameson started for Stanley Falls to make another attempt to obtain porters from Tippu Tib, who was reported to have gone to Kassongo to get men. Should this be a failure, Barttelot proposed to transfer all the baggage to the Falls, and leave it there under the care of one of the officers, while the rest of the force, with

as many armed men as Tippu Tib could be induced
for extra payment to supply, hastened up-country
in search of Stanley, whose continued absence began
to cause some uneasiness. He had told the major
verbally that, in the event of his not being overtaken
or met by the rear column, he expected to be back
at Yambuya early in November; yet by the middle
of February no word from him had reached the camp.
It was clear that he had met with some unexpected
delay.

A fortnight after Barttelot's departure, Troup,
who, during the major's absence, was in charge of the
camp, received a letter from Stanley Falls, where the
travellers had arrived on February 20th. Tippu Tib
was still absent, the date of his return was uncertain,
and till he should come back nothing could be done.
On March 24th, Barttelot returned from the Falls
without Jameson, who had gone on to Kassongo to
find Tippu Tib, and, if it could be done, hurry his
movements.

Matters were by this time worse than ever. Sixty-
seven men were dead, and Barttelot himself looked ill
and worn. Both he and Jameson had been constantly
ailing during their absence—so much so, indeed,
that the major had some suspicions that the Arabs
had tried to administer poison. However this might
be, the day after his return he was seized with a
sharp attack of fever. But he could not rest. He
had decided to send Ward down to the coast, to cable

for instructions to Sir William Mackinnon, the chair-
man of the Relief Expedition Committee, and, ill as
he was, he was anxious that Ward should start at once.

Of the wisdom of this course neither Ward nor
Troup was by any means persuaded. But whatever
their opinions might be, it was their duty to obey ;
and Troup, seeing that the major's mind was made
up, offered to escort Ward and his party overland to
Yangambi, a village on the north bank of the Congo,
some miles above the confluence of the Aruwimi.
Here they were to obtain canoes, and cross the river
to an Arab settlement at the mouth of the Lomami
River. The object of this apparently roundabout
course was to avoid the warlike Basoko villages at
the confluence of the Aruwimi, as it was quite on the
cards that the inhabitants might prove troublesome.

Ward's orders were to proceed by canoe to Bangala,
hugging the southern bank of the Congo until the
dangerous region was passed. At Bangala he was
to leave his Zanzibaris, and obtain fresh boatmen
from the Belgian station to take him to Leopoldville,
whence he was to travel overland to Matadi, and
thence by steamer to the coast. At Banana Point
he was to wait for a mail steamer, and take passage
in her either to San Thome or St. Paul de Loanda,
the two nearest points from which it was possible to
cable to Europe.

On March 28th the start was made. Long privation had so weakened the men that the difficult

journey through the forest was almost too much for them. The path was wet and slippery, and over and over again the poor fellows stumbled and fell with their loads, which they had not the power to replace on their heads. Ward and Troup were compelled to help them; and thus, travelling slowly and by short stages, the journey to Yangambi was accomplished. Crossing the Congo presented further difficulties, for the Zanzibaris were totally unacquainted with the art of managing a canoe, and it was not without considerable risk that the Lomami was finally reached.

Here Tippu Tib's nephew Raschid, who was in command, gave the travellers a friendly reception; and after Ward's departure on April 3rd, he asked Troup to wait a few days for some goats which he proposed to send to Yambuya. Ten days passed, but still the goats were not forthcoming, and Troup, unable to wait longer, set out without them. Raschid sent his own canoe to take his departing guest to Yangambi, where, to Troup's surprise, he met the major, who was on his way back to Yambuya, after a hurried trip to Stanley Falls. There had been a quarrel with some Arabs stationed near the camp; and after a day or two matters had assumed such a threatening aspect that Barttelot had rushed off to the Falls to ask for the recall of Selim, the Arab captain.

Barttelot still looked very ill, and was so excited

that his account of what had occurred was not very coherent; but he would brook no delay, and after sleeping one night at Yangambi the travellers hurried forward so rapidly that when camping-time came a good many men had lagged behind. In the morning the major again pushed on, while Troup, who was suffering from fever, and had further strained himself severely by a fall on the previous day, followed at a more leisurely pace. The journey did not improve his condition; and though for another ten days he managed to crawl about, he grew worse and worse, until on April 25th he was compelled to take to his bed.

On May 5th the steamer *A.I.A.* arrived with Lieutenant Vankerckhoven, a Free State officer, who brought the welcome news that Ward had reached Bangala in safety. The *A.I.A.* was on her way to Stanley Falls, and Vankerckhoven, having landed Ward's Zanzibaris and presented Troup with a much-needed supply of brandy, went his way, promising to pay another visit to Yambuya on his return down-stream. Meanwhile Troup, in the absence of any proper treatment, grew worse rather than better. He was entirely incapacitated, and Bonny, who was acting as doctor in charge, said that he ought to be invalided home. Barttelot was of the same opinion, and Troup, though bitterly disappointed, unwillingly concurred.

Before the steamer reappeared, Jameson, who had

at last succeeded in obtaining four hundred men to act as carriers, reached the camp. Unfortunately they were all Manyuema, and being entirely unused to porterage, had stipulated that the loads should be reduced from sixty to forty pounds each. This entailed the entire rearrangement of the baggage and the abandonment of many articles, including a considerable portion of Stanley's personal kit. These goods were shipped on board the *A.I.A.* and the *Stanley*, which arrived at Yambuya on June 4th.

Though the Manyuema had stipulated for forty-pound loads, no one supposed that a matter of a pound or two would be noticed by them. Consequently, when the loads were rearranged, some of them slightly exceeded the weight agreed, and this the men were quick to discover. They flatly refused to carry anything overweight, so the offending loads had to be reduced. But at last, on June 11th, Barttelot, Jameson, and Bonny, with their men and loads, began the long-deferred march up the Aruwimi.

Troubles speedily began. The road was bad; and the men, finding the work hard and difficult, soon began to desert, sometimes with and sometimes without their loads and rifles, while the Manyuema lost no time in proving themselves unruly. The result was that, within a few days of leaving Yambuya, the force was again subdivided—the major pushing on ahead with some of the men, while Jameson endeavoured to capture the deserters and look after the Manyuema, whose headman, Muni Somai, had insisted on halting in order to forage. Very soon it became apparent that Muni Somai's authority was only nominal—he had no real control over his men ; and when, towards the end of the month, smallpox broke out among them, the tale of misfortunes and difficulties might have seemed complete. Jameson, however, struggled manfully onward, and on June 28th succeeded in reaching the major's camp, only to find that Barttelot himself was absent on another trip to Stanley Falls. He had left directions with Bonny that Jameson should take over the command and push forward to Banalya, now an Arab station commanded by Abdallah Karoni.

To give orders was easy enough, but to carry them into effect was more difficult; and owing chiefly to the misconduct of the Manyuema, Jameson had hard work to get on at all. So slow, indeed, was his progress that he finally sent Bonny on ahead to meet the major, who had sent word that he would be at Banalya about July 14th. Bonny, with the advance guard, reached his destination on July 15th, and in due course was joined by Barttelot, who marched in from Stanley Falls.

The major had never got on well either with the Zanzibaris or the Arabs, and on the day after his arrival he fell out with Abdallah because certain expected carriers were not forthcoming. Hot words passed, and the major threatened to return to Stanley

Falls to complain to Tippu Tib. Two or three days passed, and though no carriers appeared, all went on as usual, until early on the morning of July 19th, when, in accordance with a daily custom of the Manyuema, a woman began to sing and beat a drum. The noise disturbed the major, and he sent his boy Soudi to stop it. But a further commotion at once began. Loud, angry voices were heard, and a couple of shots were fired. Barttelot then ordered some of the Sudanese to find out what was the matter, and who was shooting. At the same time he sprang out of bed, and taking his revolver, told Bonny he would shoot the first man he caught firing. Bonny tried to soothe him; but he insisted on going out, and pushing his way through to the woman who was still beating the drum, ordered her to be quiet. Scarcely were the words uttered, when her husband, a man named Sanga, fired from a neighbouring hut and shot the major dead.

Bonny ran out, and with the help of a couple of men carried the murdered man into the hut. A moment or two later a party of armed Manyuema came towards him, and fully believing that a general massacre was about to commence, he asked the leader if they were going to attack him. The man said "No;" and Bonny, having desired him to call the headmen together, induced them to have the scattered baggage collected. The last duty of that sad day was the burial of the major, and at sunset

Bonny read over him the solemn words of the Church of England burial service, and laid him to his rest under the forest trees.

Three days later Jameson, to whom Bonny had sent word of what had occurred, appeared on the scene. All was now quiet and orderly in camp, but Muni Somai and other headmen had taken their departure to Stanley Falls; and thither Jameson decided to follow them, in the hope of making some arrangement by which the expedition might be enabled to proceed. He therefore stayed at Banalya but a couple of days, in order to transact some necessary business, and on July 25th set out for the Falls.

About a week was spent in fruitless negotiations, and then, after witnessing the execution of Sanga, who had been captured by Tippu Tib's men, Jameson decided to go down the Congo to Bangala to meet Ward, of whose arrival at that station he had heard. For this purpose he obtained canoes from the Arabs, and on August 9th began his long voyage. Misfortune, however, still dogged his steps. That night he caught cold, and the next day was, as he said, " frightfully seedy." But he pushed on with indefatigable energy. On the 11th the mouth of the Aruwimi was passed; and though the chill taken two days before had developed into a severe attack of fever, he sat for hours in the hot sun engaged in soothing the natives, who had been much upset by a recent murderous raid on their villages. The following day the fever took stronger hold upon him. He became unable to touch the coarse food available, and by the 13th—the fourth day of his illness—he was in a dying condition.

His men, with the best will in the world, could do nothing for him. Their only hope lay in reaching Bangala, and with scarcely a halt they paddled on day and night, until on the 16th the weary journey ended. Ward came out to meet them, and the dying man was carried up to Vankerckhoven's hut, where for the next two days every effort was made to save him. But it was too late. His strength was worn out, and at half-past seven on the evening of the 17th, the very day of Stanley's arrival at Banalya, his brave spirit passed away.

CHAPTER XVI.

TO THE LAKE ONCE MORE.

FOR three days Stanley halted at Banalya. Then the camp was broken up, and the Manyuema were marched up the river bank, while the sick and the baggage were transported to Bungangeta Island, some miles above Banalya. There another camp was formed, and during the remainder of August the men were allowed to rest quietly and try to build up their strength. Stanley meanwhile was busily engaged in rearranging the baggage, writing reports, and interviewing the Manyuema headmen, three of whom, with their men, finally consented to accompany the expedition.

While at Stanley Falls, Jameson had written to Bonny, telling him of his intention of going to Bangala. This letter had apparently been delayed in transit, for it was not delivered until some days after the expedition reached Bungangeta. When it did arrive its contents somewhat annoyed Stanley, who was angry at the loss of his kit, and chose to consider that, in going down to Bangala, Jameson had cut himself off from the expedition. Consequently, in ignorance of Jameson's death, he wrote a sharp reply to the effect that on the day of writing (August 30th) the march would be continued. After describing the route, he went on to say that if Jameson could bring up the missing kit he was welcome to accompany the column if he could catch it up. It would, however, be unsafe to attempt the march with less than forty armed men.

Though the expedition now included a number of sick and feeble men, the advance was rapid, for the sick and the baggage were embarked in the canoes, while the path along the bank had been so far cleared that the land column encountered few obstacles. The march, however, was not without its difficulties, for smallpox was on the increase among the Manyuema, from whom it had spread also to the Madi carriers. With them, fortunately, the disease ended, for the Zanzibaris, having been vaccinated wholesale by Parke on the voyage from Zanzibar, were almost entirely immune.

As the column advanced, the natives, though keeping carefully out of sight, began to hang round in the hope of capturing stragglers. Not content with this, they next took to shooting their poisoned arrows among the men, and many, both of the land column and the canoe party, were wounded. In the majority of cases no serious effects followed, for it was found that carbonate of ammonium injected into the wound neutralized the poison ; but occasionally a vital spot was touched, and the victim fell dead before any remedy could be applied. Ulcers, too, were rather prevalent and exceedingly troublesome.

Ugarrowwa's deserted camp was reached on October 23rd. A rest would have been pleasant, but the food supply of the locality was too scanty for the luxury to be a safe one, and the column pressed forward to Andaki, where a plentiful supply of plantains was found. The fruit was not particularly large, but it was in excellent condition ; and knowing that days of scarcity lay ahead, Stanley proclaimed a halt, and issued orders that every one should dry and prepare as many plantains as he could possibly carry. The order was duly obeyed, and then the expedition passed on ; but four or five days' march beyond Andaki, Stanley noticed that some of the men, in spite of the supplies which had been gathered, began to look weak and tottery. Inquiry elicited the reply that the provisions, which should have lasted for some days, had been carelessly lost or wilfully thrown away ; and on November 7th the column was halted, in order that Uledi, with a foraging party, might go in search of food. So weak, however, had some of the people become that before they could start a few handfuls of flour for gruel had to be served out to them.

Sadly and wearily the long days of waiting wore away, but patience was at last rewarded, and on

November 10th the foragers returned with a plentiful supply. All immediate danger of famine was averted, but the time of scarcity had had its effect on the weakened frames of the men, and on the following day, when Kilonga-Longa's ferry was reached, six deaths occurred. Illness was considerably on the increase, and it was a relief to all when, on the 14th, after a sharp skirmish with the natives, a halt was called in a large clearing where remarkably fine plantains grew in profusion. Such an opportunity of making up for past deficiencies was not to be neglected, and during the three days that the column remained in camp the people gorged themselves to such an extent that, when the march was resumed, they were in no condition for work.

Food now became more plentiful, and up to a place called Ngwetza, which was reached on December 4th, there was little trouble on the score of provisions. Beyond that point, however, lay a long stretch of foodless country, and orders were issued that every man should provide himself with five days' supply. This was accordingly done; but so thoughtless and improvident were many of the people that during the first two marches many of them threw away their provisions. Consequently, on the third day these foolish fellows had nothing to eat, and that night it was decided that the sick and feeble should halt with Stanley and Bonny, while the strongest men returned to Ngwetza for supplies.

(1,153)

14

Early on December 9th the foragers set out, and for six miserable days those left behind existed rather than lived. The small supply of plantains which the more provident were able to contribute for the general support came to an end, and then a thin, weak broth made of hot water flavoured with butter and tinned milk was served out daily. It barely sufficed to keep body and soul together, and in their raging hunger many of the people wandered for miles searching for wild fruits and mushrooms.

On December 14th Bonny, in desperation, offered to take charge of the camp while Stanley returned to Ngwetza to search for the men and obtain food. To this Stanley at once agreed, and on the 15th he started with between seventy and eighty men, women, and lads, some hobbling, some almost too weak to travel, and all hungry and wretched. That night they camped supperless and miserable in the bush. But relief was at hand, for in the morning voices were heard ahead, and in a few moments the long-desired foragers appeared heavily laden with plantains. To light fires and set some of the fruit to roast was the work of a few minutes; and strengthened and refreshed by a plentiful meal, the united party hastened back to the camp. This timely supply of food brought troubles to an end; for the Ihuru lay less than one march ahead, and two days after crossing that stream the column was warmly welcomed by the Fort Bodo garrison.

Both parties had much to tell; but while Stanley's tale was of hardships and difficulties, the garrison had little but good to relate. There had been eight deaths, it was true; and at first the natives had given some trouble by their frequent raids on the plantations, where also some damage had been done by wild elephants. Then on September 1st a hurricane, accompanied by violent hail, had destroyed more than half the standing corn. But with these exceptions all had gone well.

No news had been received of either Emin or Jephson, so the only course open was to go to look for them. On December 23rd the fort, having served its purpose, was set on fire; and while the invalids and the goods, under the care of Stairs, Parke, and Bonny, were ensconced in a comfortable camp near the Ituri, Stanley, with the able-bodied of the column, began the final march to the Nyanza. This time no special difficulties were encountered, and on January 16, 1889, the camp was pitched only one long march from the lake. Here Stanley was met by letters from Emin Pasha and Jephson, which told him startling news. Some of the Egyptians had rebelled against Emin in the previous August, and he and Jephson had been made prisoners and taken to Dufflé, far up the Nile, where for some weeks they were held captive. Then a sudden turn in the affairs of the rebels led to the release of the prisoners, who, about the middle of December, had reached

Tunguru, a station on the north-west shore of the
Nyanza. Jephson's letter concluded by warning
Stanley not on any account to venture to Nsabe,
but to camp at Mbiassa's village, and thence send
word of his arrival.

To Mbiassa's village the camp was therefore
removed, and letters were dispatched to Jephson
and Emin, requesting them to come down without
loss of time, as commissariat difficulties rendered it
impossible for the expedition to halt long in the
neighbourhood. Should Emin, however, decide to
remain in the country, Stanley professed his readiness to deliver the ammunition and other stores to
any one whom the pasha might authorize to receive them.

Jephson made his appearance on February 5th,
but it was not until the 17th that the pasha arrived
with his caravan of about sixty-five persons. He
had at last made up his mind to leave the country,
though before a move could be made there was still
much to be done, and Selim Bey, one of his officers,
asked for time to bring up the soldiers and their
families from Wadelai. Stanley, of course, granted
the request, and it was arranged that Emin, with
Selim Bey and other Egyptian officers, should return
to the lake to arrange for the transport of the party.

Meanwhile Stairs, Parke, and Bonny, with their
party of convalescents, marched in from the Ituri,
and by the evening of February 18th the camp on

the plateau had developed into a well-ordered village of over five hundred inhabitants of various races and colours.

Stanley's wanderings in the Congo region were now practically ended, for it had been decided that the expedition should convoy Emin to Zanzibar by way of the Victoria Nyanza. All that remained, therefore, was to bring Emin's people and goods up from the lake; but owing to the weight and variety of the baggage, and the various delays caused by his men, this work occupied much more time than had been expected, and it was not until April 10th that the camp was finally broken up. Mazamboni's territory was reached on the 12th, and here Stanley was seized with severe internal inflammation, which at one time threatened his life, and kept the force in camp for many days. But at length he was well enough to travel, and on May 8th, Mazamboni, with three hundred of his men, escorted the expedition on the first stage of the long journey, which, nearly eight months later, finally ended at Zanzibar.

THE END.

Nelson's Books for Boys.

THE *Books below are specially suitable for Boys, and a better selection of well-written, attractively-bound, and beautifully-illustrated Gift and Prize Books cannot be found. The list may be selected from with the greatest confidence, the imprint of Messrs. Nelson being a guarantee of wholesomeness as well as of interest and general good quality.*

Many Illustrated in Colours.

THE PAGEANT OF BRITISH HISTORY.		6s. net.
	Dr. J. E. Parrott.	
"CAPTAIN SWING."	*Harold Avery.*	5s.
HOSTAGE FOR A KINGDOM.	*F. B. Forester.*	5s.
FIRELOCK AND STEEL.	*Harold Avery.*	5s.
A CAPTIVE OF THE CORSAIRS.		5s.
	John Finnemore.	
THE DUFFER.	*Warren Bell.*	5s.
A KING'S COMRADE.	*C. W. Whistler.*	5s.
IN THE TRENCHES.	*John Finnemore.*	5s.
IN JACOBITE DAYS.	*Mrs. Clarke.*	5s.
HEADS OR TAILS? (A School Story.)	*H. Avery.*	5s.
JACK RALSTON. (Life in Canada.)	*H. Burnham.*	5s.
A CAPTAIN OF IRREGULARS. (War in Chili.)		5s.
	Herbert Hayens.	

T. NELSON AND SONS, London, Edinburgh, Dublin, and New York.

NELSON'S BOOKS FOR BOYS.

IN THE GRIP OF THE SPANIARD.   5s.
Herbert Hayens.

HELD TO RANSOM. (A Story of Brigands.)   3s. 6d.
F. B. Forester.

RED, WHITE, AND GREEN. (Hungarian   3s. 6d.
Revolution.) *Herbert Hayens.*

THE TIGER OF THE PAMPAS. *H. Hayens.*   3s. 6d.

TRUE TO HIS NICKNAME. *Harold Avery.*   3s. 6d.

RED CAP. *E. S. Tylee.*   3s. 6d.

A SEA-QUEEN'S SAILING. *C. W. Whistler.*   3s. 6d.

PLAY THE GAME! *Harold Avery.*   3s. 6d.

HIGHWAY PIRATES. (A School Story.) „   3s. 6d.

SALE'S SHARPSHOOTERS. „   3s. 6d.
A rattling story of how three boys formed a very
irregular volunteer corps.

FOR KING OR EMPRESS? (Stephen and   3s. 6d.
Matilda.) *C. W. Whistler.*

SOLDIERS OF THE CROSS. *E. F. Pollard.*   3s. 6d.

TOM GRAHAM, V.C. *William Johnston.*   3s. 6d.

THE FELLOW WHO WON. *Andrew Home.*   3s. 6d.

BEGGARS OF THE SEA. *Tom Bevan.*   3s. 6d.

A TRUSTY REBEL. *Mrs. Henry Clarke.*   3s. 6d.

THE BRITISH LEGION. *Herbert Hayens.*   3s. 6d.

SCOUTING FOR BULLER. „   3s. 6d.

THE ISLAND OF GOLD. *Dr. Gordon Stables.*   3s. 6d.

HAROLD THE NORSEMAN. *Fred Whishaw.*   3s. 6d.

TOM BROWN'S SCHOOLDAYS. *Hughes.*   3s.

HEREWARD THE WAKE. *Charles Kingsley.*   3s.

T. NELSON AND SONS, London, Edinburgh, Dublin, and New York.

NELSON'S BOOKS FOR BOYS.

A LOST ARMY.	*Fred Whishaw.*	3s. 6d.
DOING AND DARING.	*Eleanor Stredder.*	3s. 6d.
BAFFLING THE BLOCKADE.		3s. 6d.
	J. Macdonald Oxley.	

THE "LONE STAR" SERIES.

Handsome Gift Books at a moderate price. Uniformly bound and well illustrated.

UNDER THE LONE STAR.	*Herbert Hayens.*	3s. 6d.
CLEVELY SAHIB.	„	3s. 6d.
AN EMPEROR'S DOOM.	„	3s. 6d.
A VANISHED NATION.	„	3s. 6d.
A FIGHTER IN GREEN.	„	3s. 6d.
THE DORMITORY FLAG.	*Harold Avery.*	3s. 6d.
KILGORMAN.	*Talbot Baines Reed.*	3s. 6d.
IN THE WILDS OF THE WEST COAST.		3s. 6d.
	J. Macdonald Oxley.	
EVERY INCH A SAILOR.	*Dr. Gordon Stables.*	3s. 6d.
AT THE POINT OF THE SWORD.		3s. 6d.
	Herbert Hayens.	
RED, WHITE, AND GREEN.	„	3s. 6d.
A HERO OF THE HIGHLANDS.	*E. E. Green.*	3s. 6d.
HELD TO RANSOM.	*F. B. Forester.*	3s. 6d.

T. NELSON AND SONS, London, Edinburgh, Dublin, and New York.

BOOKS FOR BOYS.

VICTORIES OF THE ENGINEER.   3s. 6d.
A. Williams.
Recent engineering marvels graphically described and fully illustrated.

HOW IT IS MADE.   *A. Williams.*   3s. 6d.

HOW IT WORKS.   „   3s. 6d.
Splendid books for boys, telling them just what they want to know. Profusely illustrated.

IN FLORA'S REALM.   *Edward Step, F.L.S.*   3s. 6d.

A NATURALIST'S HOLIDAY. „   „   3s. 6d.
Two books by one of the most popular of living writers on natural history subjects.

THE "ACTIVE SERVICE" SERIES.

FOR THE COLOURS.   *Herbert Hayens.*   2s. 6d.
A Boy's Book of the Army.

YE MARINERS OF ENGLAND.   2s. 6d.
Herbert Hayens.
A Boy's Book of the Navy.

TRAFALGAR REFOUGHT.   2s. 6d.
Sir W. Laird Clowes and Alan H. Burgoyne.

AUTOBIOGRAPHY OF A SEAMAN.   2s. 6d.
Abridged from Lord Dundonald.

ADVENTURES IN THE RIFLE BRIGADE.   2s. 6d.
Sir John Kincaid.

ROMANCE AND REALM OF COMMERCE.   *net* 2s.
Alfred Morris.
This is a capital book for boys, pointing out the advantages and attractions of a business career as compared with the professions, etc. Just the thing to give to a boy entering or about to choose a business.

T. NELSON AND SONS, London, Edinburgh, Dublin, and New York.

NELSON'S BOOKS FOR BOYS.

THE GOLD KLOOF.	*H. A. Bryden.*	2s. 6d.
SEA DOGS ALL!	*Tom Bevan.*	2s. 6d.
THE FEN ROBBERS.	"	2s. 6d.
RED DICKON, THE OUTLAW.	"	2s. 6d.
HAVELOK THE DANE.	*Charles W. Whistler.*	2s. 6d.
KING ALFRED'S VIKING.	"	2s. 6d.
THE VANISHED YACHT.	*Harcourt Burrage.*	2s. 6d.
A splendid story of adventure.		
MY STRANGE RESCUE.	*J. Macdonald Oxley.*	2s. 6d.
DIAMOND ROCK.	"	2s. 6d.
UP AMONG THE ICE-FLOES.	"	2s. 6d.
CHUMS AT LAST.	*Mrs. G. Forsyth Grant.*	2s. 6d.
MOBSLEY'S MOHICANS. (A Tale of Two Terms.)		2s. 6d.
	Harold Avery.	
KNIGHTS OF THE ROAD.	*E. Everett-Green.*	2s. 6d.
ROBINSON CRUSOE.	*Defoe.*	2s. 6d.
WON IN WARFARE.	*C. R. Kenyon.*	2s. 6d.
THE WIZARD'S WAND.	*Harold Avery.*	2s. 6d.
A PRINCE ERRANT.	*C. W. Whistler.*	2s. 6d.
BRAVE MEN AND BRAVE DEEDS.		2s. 6d.
	M. B. Synge.	
RALPH THE OUTLAW.	*Mrs. H. Clarke.*	2s.
THE "GREY FOX."	*Tom Bevan.*	2s.
THE JEWELLED LIZARD.	*W. D. Fordyce.*	2s.

T. NELSON AND SONS, London, Edinburgh, Dublin, and New York.

Books for the Young.

NELSON'S "ROYAL" LIBRARIES

THE finest and most attractive series of Gift and Reward Books in the market at so moderate a price. They are mainly COPYRIGHT works, carefully selected from the most popular and successful of the many books for the young issued by Messrs. Nelson in recent years, and are most attractively illustrated and tastefully bound. Each volume has eight coloured plates, with the exception of a few, which have eight monochrome illustrations. The books are issued in three series at 2/-, 1/6, and 1/-. For lists see following pages.

THOMAS NELSON AND SONS,
London, Edinburgh, Dublin, and New York.

NELSON'S "ROYAL" LIBRARIES.

THE TWO SHILLING SERIES.

VERA'S TRUST.	*E. Everett-Green.*
FOR THE FAITH	*E. Everett-Green.*
ALISON WALSH.	*Constance Evelyn.*
BLIND LOYALTY.	*E. L. Haverfield.*
DOROTHY ARDEN.	*J. M. Callwell.*
FALLEN FORTUNES.	*E. Everett-Green.*
FOR HER SAKE.	*Gordon Roy.*
JACK MACKENZIE.	*Gordon Stables, M.D.*
IN PALACE AND FAUBOURG.	*C. J. G.*
ISABEL'S SECRET; or, A Sister's Love.	
IVANHOE.	*Sir Walter Scott.*
KENILWORTH.	*Sir Walter Scott.*
LÉONIE.	*Annie Lucas.*
MAUD MELVILLE'S MARRIAGE.	*E. Everett-Green.*
OLIVE ROSCOE.	*E. Everett-Green.*
QUEECHY.	*Miss Wetherell.*
SCHÖNBERG-COTTA FAMILY.	*Mrs. Charles.*
"SISTER."	*E. Everett-Green.*
THE CITY AND THE CASTLE.	*Annie Lucas.*
THE CZAR.	*Deborah Alcock.*
THE HEIRESS OF WYLMINGTON.	*Everett-Green.*
THE SIGN OF THE RED CROSS.	*Everett-Green.*
THE SPANISH BROTHERS.	*Deborah Alcock.*
THE TRIPLE ALLIANCE.	*Harold Avery.*
THE UNCHARTED ISLAND.	*Skelton Kuppord.*
THE WIDE WIDE WORLD.	*Miss Wetherell.*

T. NELSON AND SONS, London, Edinburgh, Dublin, and New York.

NELSON'S "ROYAL" LIBRARIES.

THE EIGHTEENPENCE SERIES.

IN LIONLAND.	*M. Douglas.*
MARGIE AT THE HARBOUR LIGHT.	*E. A. Rand.*
ADA AND GERTY.	*Louisa M. Gray.*
AFAR IN THE FOREST.	*W. H. G. Kingston.*
A GOODLY HERITAGE.	*K. M. Eady.*
BORIS THE BEAR HUNTER.	*Fred Whishaw.*
"DARLING."	*M. H. Cornwall Legh.*
DULCIE'S LITTLE BROTHER.	*E. Everett-Green.*
ESTHER'S CHARGE.	*E. Everett-Green.*
EVER HEAVENWARD.	*Mrs. Prentiss.*
FOR THE QUEEN'S SAKE.	*E. Everett-Green.*
GUY POWERS' WATCHWORD.	*J. T. Hopkins.*
IN THE ROCKY MOUNTAINS.	*W. H. G. Kingston.*
IN THE WARS OF THE ROSES.	*E. Everett-Green.*
LIONEL HARCOURT, THE ETONIAN.	*G. E. Wyatt.*
MOLLY'S HEROINE.	*"Fleur de Lys."*
NORSELAND TALES.	*H. H. Boyesen.*
ON ANGELS' WINGS.	*Hon. Mrs. Greene.*
ONE SUMMER BY THE SEA.	*J. M. Callwell.*
PARTNERS.	*H. F. Gethen.*
ROBINETTA.	*L. E. Tiddeman.*
SALOME.	*Mrs. Marshall.*
THE LORD OF DYNEVOR.	*E. Everett-Green.*
THE YOUNG HUGUENOTS.	*"Fleur de Lys."*
THE YOUNG RAJAH.	*W. H. G. Kingston.*
WINNING THE VICTORY.	*E. Everett-Green.*

T. NELSON AND SONS, London, Edinburgh, Dublin, and New York.

NELSON'S "ROYAL" LIBRARIES.

THE SHILLING SERIES.

AMPTHILL TOWERS. *A. J. Foster.*
IVY AND OAK.
ARCHIE DIGBY. *G. E. Wyatt.*
AS WE SWEEP THROUGH THE DEEP.
Gordon Stables, M.D.
AT THE BLACK ROCKS. *Edward Rand.*
AUNT SALLY. *Constance Milman.*
CYRIL'S PROMISE. A Temperance Tale. *W. J. Lacey.*
GEORGIE MERTON. *Florence Harrington.*
GREY HOUSE ON THE HILL. *Hon. Mrs. Greene.*
HUDSON BAY. *R. M. Ballantyne.*
JUBILEE HALL. *Hon. Mrs. Greene.*
LOST SQUIRE OF INGLEWOOD. *Dr. Jackson.*
MARK MARKSEN'S SECRET. *Jessie Armstrong.*
MARTIN RATTLER. *R. M. Ballantyne.*
RHODA'S REFORM. *M. A. Paull.*
SHENAC. The Story of a Highland Family in Canada.
SIR AYLMER'S HEIR. *E. Everett-Green.*
SOLDIERS OF THE QUEEN. *Harold Avery.*
THE CORAL ISLAND. *R. M. Ballantyne.*
THE DOG CRUSOE. *R. M. Ballantyne.*
THE GOLDEN HOUSE. *Mrs. Woods Baker.*
THE GORILLA HUNTERS. *R. M. Ballantyne.*
THE ROBBER BARON. *A. J. Foster.*
THE WILLOUGHBY BOYS. *Emily C. Hartley.*
UNGAVA. *R. M. Ballantyne.*
WORLD OF ICE. *R. M. Ballantyne.*
YOUNG FUR TRADERS. *R. M. Ballantyne.*

T. NELSON AND SONS, London, Edinburgh, Dublin, and New York.